200 Crochet blocks

200 Crochet blocks

for blankets, throws and afghans

JAN EATON

sewandso

A SEWANDSO BOOK

SewandSo is an imprint of F&W Media International, Ltd
Pynes Hill Court, Pynes Hill, Exeter, EX2 5AZ, UK

F&W Media International, Ltd is a subsidiary of F+W Media, Inc
10151 Carver Road, Suite #200, Blue Ash, OH 45242, USA

First published in the UK in 2004 by F&W Media International, Ltd
Pynes Hill Court, Pynes Hill, Exeter, EX2 5AZ, UK

A catalogue record for this book is available from the British Library.

ISBN 0 7153 2141 2

Conceived, designed, and produced by
Quarto Publishing plc
The Old Brewery
6 Blundell Street
London N7 9BH

QUAR.ABL

Project Editor Jo Fisher
Senior Art Editor Sally Bond
Designer Jo Long
Copy Editor Hazel Williams
Photographer Colin Bowling
Illustrator Coral Mula
Proofreader Jan Eaton, Sally Maceachern
Indexer Pamela Ellis
Art Director Moira Clinch
Publisher Piers Spence

Manufactured by Universal Graphics, Singapore
Printed in China by 1010 Printing International Ltd

25 24 23 22 21 20 19 18

F&W Media publishes high quality books on a wide range of subjects.
For more great book ideas visit:
www.sewandso.co.uk

Contents

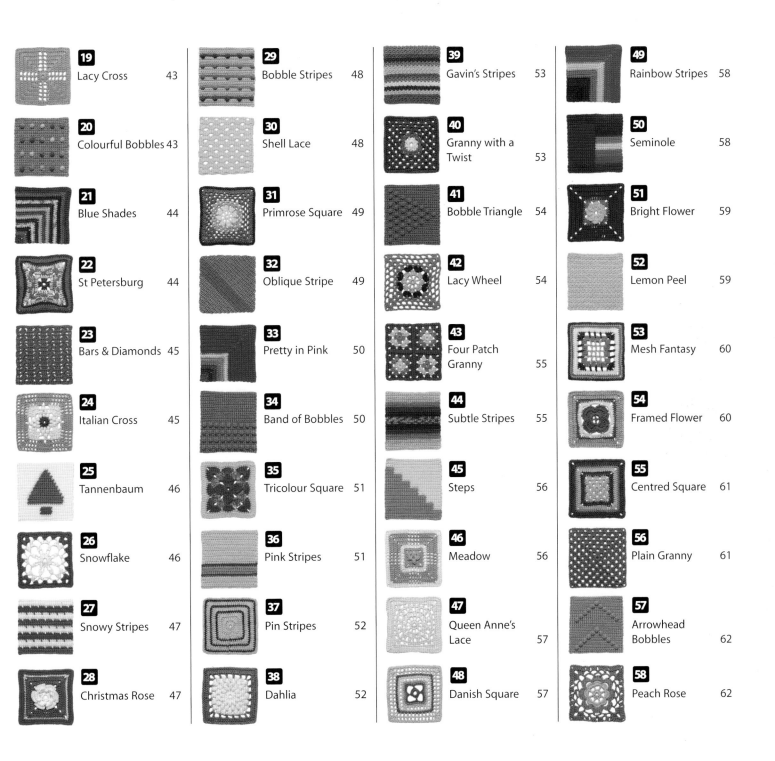

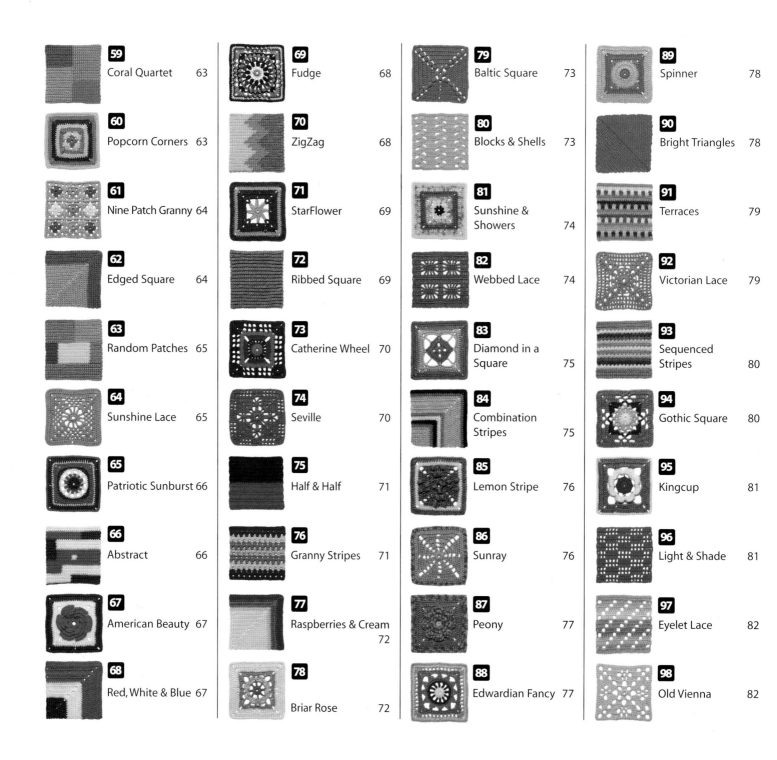

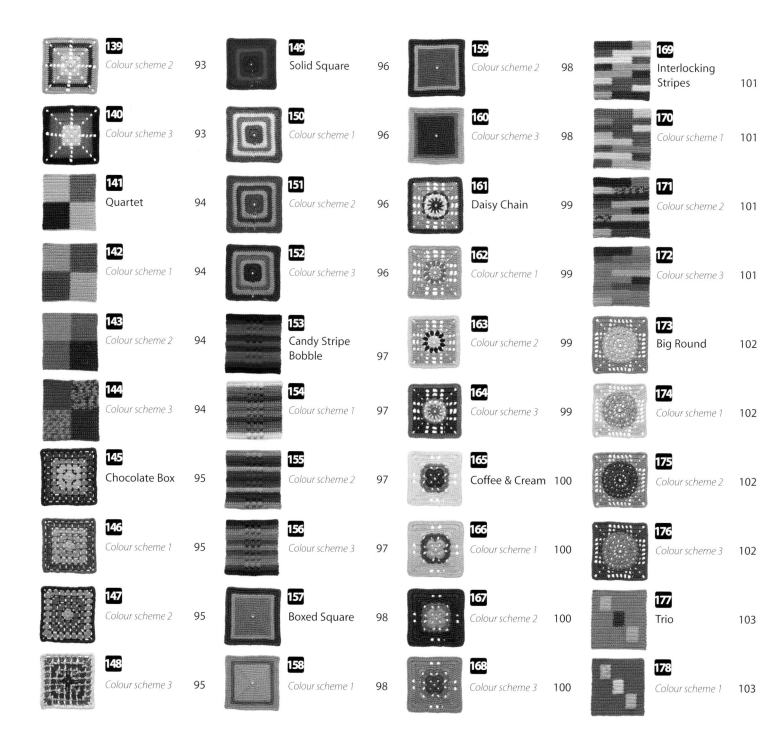

Tricolour Square, block 35

Introduction

Crochet is one of the oldest and most fascinating ways of creating a fabric with yarn. By using a hook to work loops with a continuous length of yarn, it's easy to produce a fabric with endless variations of texture, pattern and colour. Making small blocks out of crochet and joining them together to make a larger piece of fabric has long been a favourite way of working and incorporating odds and ends of yarn. Breaking a large piece of crochet down in small, easily transportable units means you can crochet blocks on a bus, train, or plane journey, as well as while watching television or listening to music or audio books. The author has been crocheting since she was a small child and finds picking up a ball of yarn and a hook and settling down to crochet the perfect way to unwind after a long stressful day. She is an avid collector of old crochet patterns and magazines and has reworked many traditional designs to make some of the blocks in the book, as well as creating many of the block patterns herself. After working more than 200 different blocks over the last few months, she is still as intrigued by the craft as ever.

Colours and yarns

The colours and yarns used to work each block are the author's own personal choice. It can't be stressed strongly enough that the patterns can be worked using any colours and combinations of colours that you prefer. Some useful guidelines about choosing and using colour (page 20) are included and it is hoped

Lacy Cross, block 19

Bobble Stripes, block 29

Alhambra, block 14

that these will help you enjoy exploring the whole spectrum of coloured yarns that are available. The author prefers working with a smooth, pure wool yarn. She has chosen to use double knitting (DK weight) yarn for all the blocks for several reasons—it is a good thickness to work with and shows up the different stitches well. It was also necessary to ensure that the blocks would be the same size when finished, so they can be mixed and joined without difficulty. Double knitting (DK weight) yarn also has the advantage of being available in a wonderful range of colours.

Wisteria, block 113

However, you should feel free to use whatever yarn suits you, whether it's made from wool, cotton, a synthetic fibre such as acrylic or a wool/synthetic blend. Always keep to the same weight of yarn throughout a project.

Combining blocks

As well as patterns for making over 200 blocks, a selection of block combinations is included to give you inspiration when arranging blocks to make throws, afghans and cushion covers. The designs will provide you with a useful jumping-off point and encourage you to begin combining blocks in new and unusual ways. The author's aim is to inspire both new and experienced crafters to take on the challenge of designing and making their own personal, unique piece of crochet and transform the humble afghan into a wonderful and desirable item for the traditional or modern home.

Floral Fantasy, page 29

How to use this book

At the beginning of this book you'll find an illustrated contents list showing you photographs of all the main blocks—these are cross-referenced, according to the techniques used and the degree of difficulty of the pattern, from beginner to advanced. Look through and find one you like that matches your skill level.

Mix and Match

The Mix and Match section, pages 14-31, takes you through the process of creating your own afghan design, giving you advice on combining blocks, mixing techniques, and exploring the world of colour. There are also plans for making 12 afghans, throws and cushion covers using a selection of blocks from the book. They include large designs, as well as small, quick-to-make designs.

SIZE
All the blocks are the same size, 15cm (6") square, and have been worked using the same weight of yarn and size of hook, so any block can be mixed and matched with others at will.

READING THE PLANS
Each afghan plan is accompanied by details of the finished size of the item, the type of yarn, colours and hook size, as well as the names and reference numbers of the component blocks and how many to make of each one. This section also tells you how to finish off your blocks and join them together, and suggests a suitable edging to finish off your project.

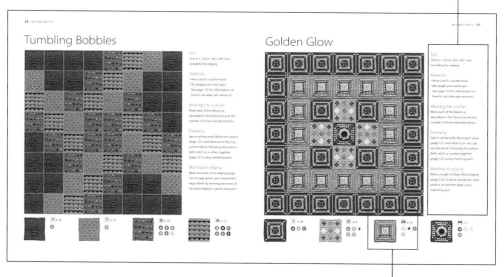

TURNING THE BLOCKS
Some of the blocks used in the plans need to be turned clockwise or counterclockwise by 90° or 180° to make up the design. When assembling your blocks, check the plan carefully and make sure the colour and pattern within each block matches the plan.

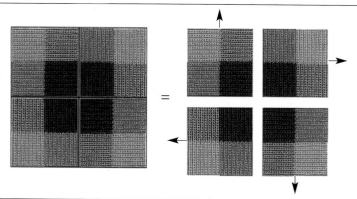

200 x 16

Ⓐ Ⓑ Ⓒ
Ⓓ

QUANTITY & COLOURS
Each block used for the design is shown below the plan, accompanied by its pattern reference number, yarn colours and how many of that block you need to make.

The Block Directory

The afghan Block Directory contains a wide variety of block patterns, from well-loved traditional patterns to brand-new designs. Each block is accompanied by a photograph, pattern instructions, yarn colours and helpful symbols. The Block Directory is divided into two sections. Section one (pages 34 to 83) contains patterns for 100 blocks, while section two (pages 84 to 111), includes more than 100 blocks and explores alternative colour combinations.

Techniques

The final section of this book contains detailed information on the abbreviations and how to work the stitches and techniques used. Different methods of joining blocks are demonstrated, as well as patterns for a selection of edgings to finish off your projects beautifully. At the end of the section, there are tips on choosing yarns and a list of the actual yarns used in this book.

122 Ⓐ Ⓑ Ⓒ Ⓓ

The second section of the book shows different colour combinations for each block. Each yarn colour is clearly referenced as used in the accompanying pattern.

PAGES 34-83

PAGES 84-111

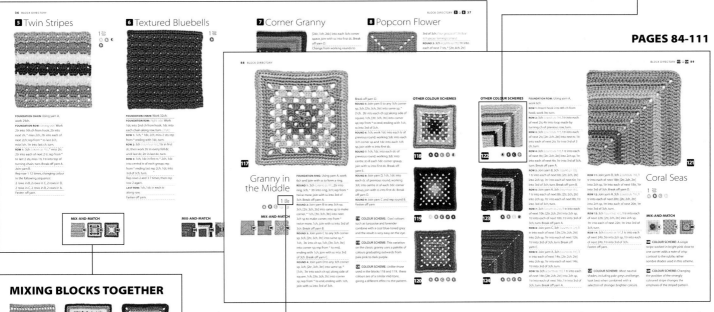

MIXING BLOCKS TOGETHER

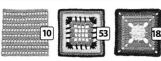

You can use your own imagination to mix blocks or experiment with the recommendations here.

UNDERSTANDING THE SYMBOLS

Each block pattern is accompanied by one or more symbols indicating how each pattern is worked, and a symbol indicating the pattern's degree of difficulty:

⮂ **WORKED IN ROWS**
This symbol shows that the block has been worked backward and forward in rows.

◐ **WORKED IN ROUNDS**
This symbol is used for blocks worked in the round from the centre outward. You will find some blocks, for example block 53 Mesh Fantasy, are accompanied by both symbols as they have part of the pattern worked in rows and part in rounds.

LEVEL OF DIFFICULTY

1 Beginner blocks

11 Some experience required

111 Challenging

Mix and Match

This chapter shows you how to choose and combine blocks from the directory and includes a selection of colourful design ideas for making items in various sizes from a large throw to a cushion cover plus tips on how to plan your own design. A further section explores selecting and using your own choice of colour.

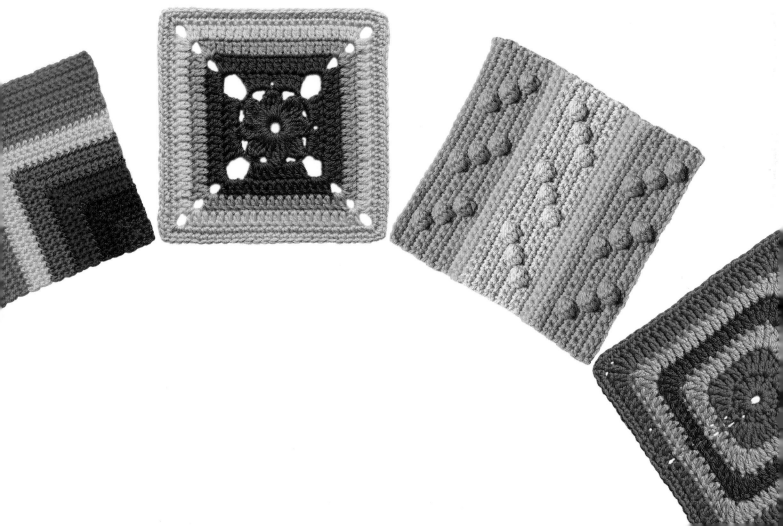

Mixing and matching blocks

Choosing blocks

All the 212 blocks in the Block Directory are the same size, 15cm (6") square, so there are thousands of possible combinations you could put together when designing your own afghan, throw or pillow cover. The size of your finished project depends on its use—a throw to cover a double bed will need to be much larger than an everyday afghan for you to snuggle into when reading or watching television. You can work to whatever size feels comfortable for you; for example, a 107cm (42") or 122cm (48") square afghan is a good, all-purpose size for throwing over a sofa or chair. If you find the idea of working to this size too daunting or time consuming, you can put together the blocks to make an 45cm (18") square cushion cover in a few evenings.

On pages 22 to 31, in the Mix and Match section, you'll find 12 colourful designs, in various sizes, including a large throw called Eastern Promise (page 25), which measures 180cm by 210cm (72" by 84"), and a 91cm (36") square baby blanket called Pastel Rainbow (page 31). As well as working the designs as they are shown, you can change the yarn colours to suit your own tastes—for more information, refer to Using Colours, pages 20 and 21. You can also use the block arrangements to inspire you to begin mixing blocks and creating your very own original afghan. Begin by looking through the Block Directory (pages 32 to 111) and choose several blocks that appeal to you and are suitable for your current skill level. The degree of difficulty symbols, which accompany each block, are explained on page 13. Don't forget that you don't have to choose the same yarn colours used by the author when working the blocks.

Planning your design

When designing a piece made out of crochet blocks, it's a good idea to make a visual plan, to make sure you'll be happy with your finished item. You can make a plan very simply by marking out the outline of the required number of blocks on graph paper to make a grid of squares. Make each block about 2.5cm (1") square on the graph paper. Colour the squares with pencils, or felt-tipped pens, in the colours and patterns of the blocks you have chosen.

Another way is to crochet one of each type of block you intend to use, then take the blocks to your local photocopy shop and get several copies of each one reduced to a smaller size, say about 4cm (1 ½") square. You can do this yourself at home if you have access to a computer, printer and scanner.

Cut out the copies and arrange them on a large sheet of plain paper. Move the blocks around until you're happy with the arrangement, then either tape them down or stick them in place using a glue stick. At the side of your plan, attach a copy of each block and write down the number you need to make and details of the colours you have chosen. There's information on page 125 telling you how to calculate the amounts of yarn you will need to buy.

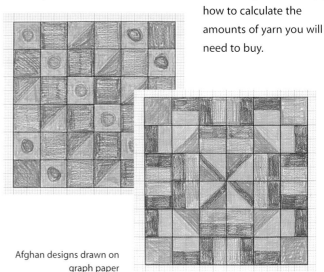

Afghan designs drawn on graph paper

Combining blocks

Crochet fabric can be smooth, lacy or textured, depending on which technique you are using. Blocks can be worked in rows or in rounds and each way of working has its own visual appeal—for example, compare block 29 Bobble Stripes with block 55 Centred Square. Each block is worked in a similar colour scheme, but the two look completely different. You can combine blocks at random just because you like their appearance or use a more measured approach. Look at the Floral Fantasy design on page 29 as an example of combining blocks worked in rounds together. Here, a strong checkerboard pattern, made with block 189 Willow, provides the perfect framework to show off paler blocks worked in shades of pink. Similarly, the Golden Glow design (page 27) combines blocks worked in the round, but this design builds outward from one central square.

LACE BLOCKS

Lace blocks work well when they are combined with each other, but they can also be used to add a touch of lightness to other block combinations. Lace blocks make perfect baby afghans, as the crochet

Worked in rows — Worked in rounds

Smooth — Lacy — Textured

Think about the different textures and methods of working blocks when deciding which to combine

fabric is soft and tends to drape well, whether used as a cot or pram cover or a shawl for wrapping baby. The author likes combining lace blocks with heavier, more closely worked ones but when doing this, you should bear in mind that not only the weight and density of individual blocks will be different but the amount of stretch and drape will vary too.

TEXTURED BLOCKS

Textured blocks combine well with each other, whether they are plain or patterned. Textures add surface interest to bold, modern designs, such as Deco Delight (page 23), where patterns of bobbles break up the large areas of plain colour. The design on page 26, Tumbling Bobbles, shows how effective textured blocks in solid colours can be when combined with a small number of multicoloured blocks.

Golden Glow, page 27—combines various blocks worked in rounds

Creating patterns

Different patterns start to appear when you arrange identical blocks into groups of four or more and start turning some of the blocks in different directions. For example, take a simple block made from two identical triangles *(block 90 Bright Triangles)* and see how many combinations you can make using four or more blocks.

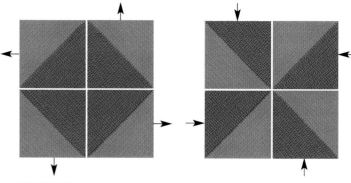

SAWTOOTH

Four blocks placed as shown above make a sawtooth pattern. This could be repeated across a whole afghan using colours that shade gradually into each other—think dark and light blues rippling into shades of mauve and pink.

DIAMOND

Create a simple, yet visually effective diamond shape by starting with the top right block the correct way up, then turning the other blocks 90° away from each other in turn.

WINDMILL

Form a windmill pattern by starting with the bottom right block the correct way up, then turning the other blocks 90° away from each other in turn.

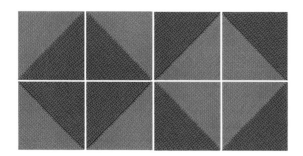

DIAMOND COMBINATIONS

Next to the first diamond, place a second made by turning individual blocks so that the diamond is now made from the background colour *(left)*. Add two more four-block groups below the first two and you've got the beginning of an interesting repeat pattern *(right)*. This way of working with geometric shapes is very similar to making patchwork blocks out of fabric and you'll find lots of inspiration in books of traditional quilt block patterns.

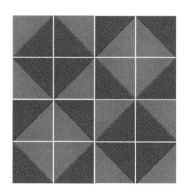

STRIPES

Striped blocks also offer a range of design possibilities. Using the simplest striped block in the book, block 75 Half & Half, arrange several with the top edges facing the same way, to make narrow horizontal or vertical stripes *(right)*, then turn one row to create a wider stripe *(far right)*.

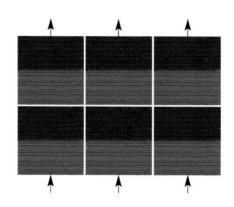

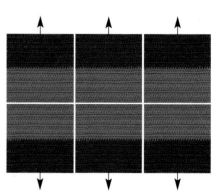

BROKEN STRIPES

Broken stripe patterns are made by alternating the top and bottom of each block *(right)* or by turning some blocks vertically *(below)*.

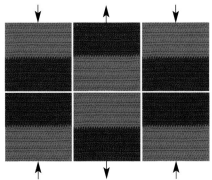

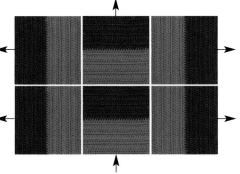

STEPPED ZIGZAG

One of the nicest patterns made with striped blocks is a stepped zigzag, made by turning alternate blocks vertically and horizontally *(right)*. The patterns you can make will also vary depending on the width and complexity of the stripes on the actual block you choose.

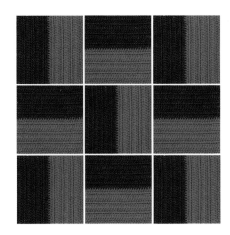

CREATING FRAMES

Striped blocks combined with corner blocks in matching or coordinating colours are useful as a way of making a "frame" around an afghan *(blocks 187 and 194 shown left)*.

Edgings

A compatible edging finishes off any piece of crochet made from blocks. Plain or striped rows of double crochet edging (page 122) look nice if you like a simple, straight edge, but for something more ornate choose one of the edging patterns on pages 122 to 123. The edgings shown on these pages are all worked in narrow rows across the width so it's easy to make the exact length of edging you need. Don't forget that you'll need to make the edging a little longer to stretch around the corners neatly—you can gather, pleat or fold the edging strip into the corners, so that the strip lies flat without pulling. As a rule, apply an edging neatly by stitching it in place with yarn that matches the edging in colour.

Looking after afghans

Afghans look wonderful used as bed, chair or sofa throws and they add warmth, as well as decoration, to any room. Spruce up a plain, neutral décor with an afghan in bright, lively colours, or coordinate your throw with the existing colour scheme. Baby afghans are popular items to make and give as presents.

Always clean your afghan regularly, according to the care instructions on the ball band of the yarns you have used. You may prefer to have very large throws and afghans professionally dry-cleaned. To store afghans not in use, never enclose them in a plastic bag, as the fibres will not be able to breathe and the static cling created by polythene will attract dust and dirt. Instead, wrap in a clean cotton pillowcase or sheet, depending on size. Store in a dry, cool, dust-free place, adding a bag of dried lavender to keep the crochet smelling sweet and to deter moths.

Using colours

There are no hard and fast rules governing the use of colour in a crochet design—all colours combine and interact in different ways, some of which may appear more, or less pleasing to the eye. The most important thing to remember is that colour is a very personal thing, so you could start exploring colour by experimenting with colours that you find initially appealing. The range of colours you choose for your clothes and home decorations will give you a clear indication of your own colour preferences. For example, you may like subtle shades of blue, but think red and orange are bright and garish, or love dark colours, such as black and brown, but dislike pale neutral shades.

Colour palettes

A good way to begin exploring the wonderful world of colour is to make your own personal colour palette. Cut a strip of thin white card about 8cm x 30cm (3" x 12") and punch a row of holes along one long edge. Collect a selection of yarns in colours that you know you like and loop a short length of each one through alternate holes. Now it's time to add some spice to your palette with different colours of yarn, adding new lengths gradually, one colour at a time, to see what effect they create. For example, if you prefer pastel shades, see what happens when you combine deeper, brighter versions of your well-loved colours—try adding cobalt or royal blue to your favourite

Colour palettes: the one on the left shows cool pastel and bright colours, while the right one shows neutrals and warm shades

powder blue; fuchsia or bright raspberry pink to pale baby pinks and creams; emerald and strong lime green to eau-de-nil.

You may have an instinctive feeling for warm colours (for example, yellow, mustard, red, tan) or cool ones (lavender, blue, green, turquoise, blue grey) or you may prefer light-toned, pastel shades to strong, bright or dark ones. Some colours (pink, for example) can be either warm or cool, depending on the particular shade you choose—peachy pinks are warm, as they contain some yellow, which is a warm colour, while fuchsia pinks tend to be cool, as they contain blue, a cool colour.

Colour theory

A few basic colour theory guidelines are useful to consider at this stage. Investigate the standard wheel arrangement of colours, where the three primary colours, red, yellow and blue, are divided by the three secondary colours (orange, green and purple), which are made by mixing two primary colours together. Generally, colours opposite each other on the colour wheel (these are called complementary colours, for example, red and green) may clash with each other when used at full strength. Neighbouring colours on the wheel, such as blue and purple, are usually harmonious, as they each contain some of the same colour.

In general, warm colours tend to advance while cool colours tend to recede. The same is true with dark and light tones of the same colour—dark tones tend to advance and light tones to recede. This effect can totally alter the appearance of a block pattern—see pages 84-111 for examples of how a block pattern varies when it is worked in four different colour schemes. Individual colours also change according to how they are placed in a block. An area of scarlet surrounded by black or navy blue will look bold and striking, while the same scarlet area surrounded by white, pale grey or cream will have less impact. By introducing more brightly coloured areas into the block, the initial impact of the scarlet area will be diminished. Similarly, stripes and small areas of black or dark brown can enhance a design, defining and accentuating the pattern. This works in the same way as the black leaded lines in a stained glass window that surround brilliantly coloured glass shapes and create a glowing jewel-like effect.

Warm colours

Cool colours

Different colour combinations of the same design (see pages 84–111)

Blocks with different designs but using similar or complementary colours

Creative colour

When choosing your own colours to work a crochet block, you may need to crochet more than one sample, as the colours may create a different effect when they are combined from the one you anticipated. It's interesting to see how different yarn colours in skeins or balls may look good when placed together, but the colours often change and react with each other when the yarns are combined in a piece of crochet.

Inspiration for colour

For more inspiration and help with colour, start by looking at the wide range of colour-mixing books for water colourists and oil painters. They often include colour suggestions for painting landscapes and interiors, when the painter wants to create a particular season or time of day.

Look around you at flowers, plants, gardens and the colours of birds, animals and insects. View paintings and other works of art in museums and galleries and look at how different colours have been put together and what effect they create. For example, Tiffany glass and works by the Art Nouveau movement utilize different colour palettes from the vibrant colours favored by America's Jazz Age and Art Deco Style. Hot African colours are very different from the restrained palette used in Japanese woodcuts by Hokusai and Hiroshige. Other beautifully coloured museum objects to look at include Oriental textiles, particularly Japanese kimonos, and jewelry made from gems and semi-precious stones. Keep a scrapbook and paste into it anything that appeals to you colourwise—postcards, magazine cuttings, paint samples, swatches of fabric and thread are all useful as reference.

Find colour inspiration in nature or works of art

Mix and match designs
Blue Horizons

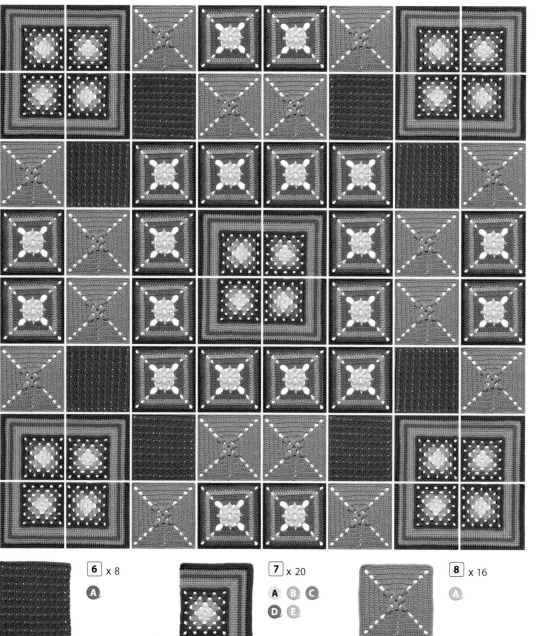

Size:
122cm x 122cm (48" x 48") not including the edging.

Materials:
- 4mm (size F) crochet hook
- DK weight pure wool yarn
  See page 125 for information on how to calculate yarn amounts.

Working the crochet:
Work each of the blocks as described in the Directory and the number of times indicated below.

Finishing:
Sew in all the ends. Block each piece (page 121) and allow to dry. Lay out the blocks following the pattern (left), stitch or crochet together (page 121) using matching yarn.

Working an edging:
Work a length of Shamrock Edging (page 122) in cornflower blue yarn and stitch it around the edge using matching yarn.

6 x 8
A

7 x 20
A B C
D E

8 x 16
A

182 x 20
A B C
D E

Deco Delight

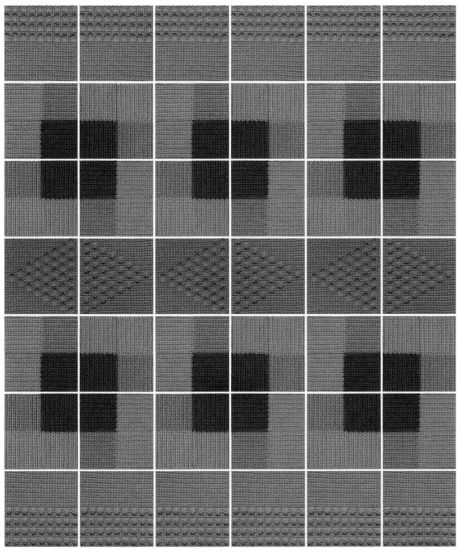

Size:
91cm x 106cm (36" x 42") not including the edging.

Materials:
• 4mm (size F) crochet hook
• DK weight pure wool yarn
  See page 125 for information on how to calculate yarn amounts.

Working the crochet:
Work each of the blocks as described in the Directory and the number of times indicated below.

Finishing:
Sew in all the ends. Block each piece (page 121) and allow to dry. Lay out the blocks following the pattern (left), stitch or crochet together (page 121) using matching yarn.

Working an edging:
Work two rows of dc edging (page 122) in fuchsia yarn around the edge.

 34 x 12
A

 41 x 6
A

 143 x 24
A B C
D

Waterlily Pond

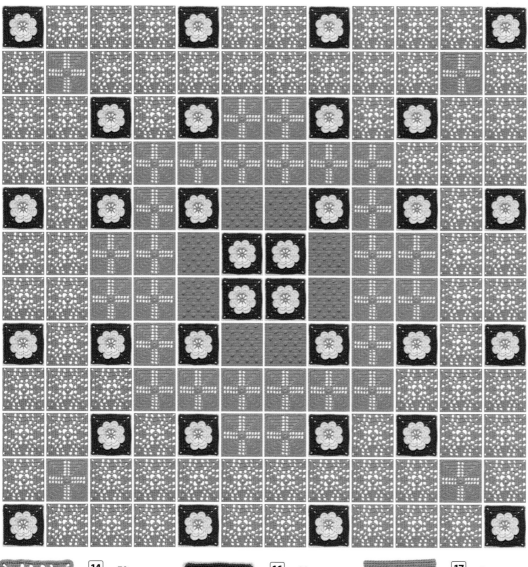

Size:
180cm x 180cm (72" x 72") not including the edging.

Materials:
- 4mm (size F) crochet hook
- DK weight pure wool yarn
  See page 125 for information on how to calculate yarn amounts.

Working the crochet:
Work each of the blocks as described in the Directory and the number of times indicated below.

Finishing:
Sew in all the ends. Block each piece (page 121) and allow to air dry. Lay out the blocks following the pattern (left), stitch or crochet together (page 121) using matching yarn.

Working an edging:
To make a simple, narrow edging, work two rows of dc edging (page 122) in cream yarn around the edge. Alternatively, work a length of Shell and Lace Edging (page 123) in clover pink or cream yarn and stitch it around the edge using matching yarn.

 14 x 72
A

 16 x 32
A B C

17 x 8
A

  19 x 32
A

Eastern Promise

Size:
180cm x 210cm (72" x 84") not including the edging.

Materials:
- 4mm (size F) crochet hook
- DK weight pure wool yarn
  See page 125 for information on how to calculate yarn amounts

Working the crochet:
Work each of the blocks as described in the Directory and the number of times indicated below.

Finishing:
Sew in all the ends. Block each piece (page 121) and allow to air dry. Lay out the blocks following the pattern (left), stitch or crochet together (page 121) using matching yarn.

Working an edging:
Work two dc edging rows (page 122) in amethyst yarn and then another two dc edging rows in raspberry yarn.

13 x 44

15 x 124

Tumbling Bobbles

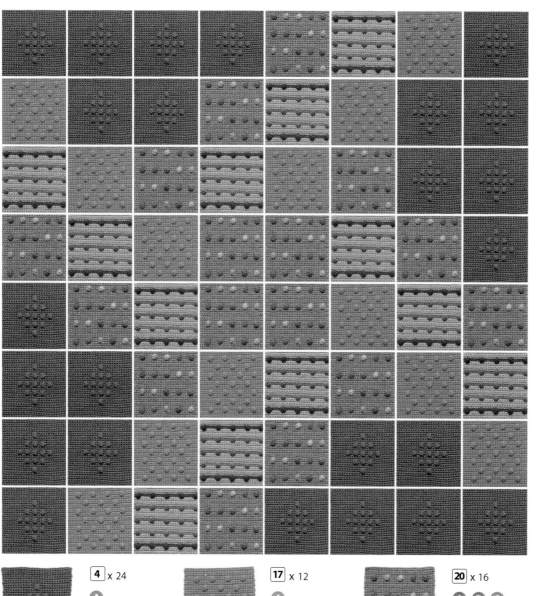

Size:
122cm x 122cm (48" x 48") not including the edging.

Materials:
- 4mm (size F) crochet hook
- DK weight pure wool yarn
  See page 125 for information on how to calculate yarn amounts.

Working the crochet:
Work each of the blocks as described in the Directory and the number of times indicated below.

Finishing:
Sew in all the ends. Block each piece (page 121) and allow to air dry. Lay out the blocks following the pattern (left), stitch or crochet together (page 121) using matching yarn.

Working an edging:
Work two rows of dc edging (page 122) in sage green yarn around the edge. Finish by working two rows of the same edging in petrol blue yarn.

 4 x 24
 17 x 12
 20 x 16
 29 x 12

Golden Glow

Size:
107cm x 107cm (42" x 42") not including the edging.

Materials:
- 4mm (size F) crochet hook
- DK weight pure wool yarn
  See page 125 for information on how to calculate yarn amounts.

Working the crochet:
Work each of the blocks as described in the Directory and the number of times indicated below.

Finishing:
Sew in all the ends. Block each piece (page 121) and allow to air dry. Lay out the blocks following the pattern (left), stitch or crochet together (page 121) using matching yarn.

Working an edging:
Work a length of Deep Mesh Edging (page 122) in burnt orange yarn and stitch it around the edge using matching yarn.

 3 x 28

 A B C

 61 x 4

 A B C
D E

 200 x 16

 A B C
D

 209 x 1

 A B C
D

Stripes & Squares

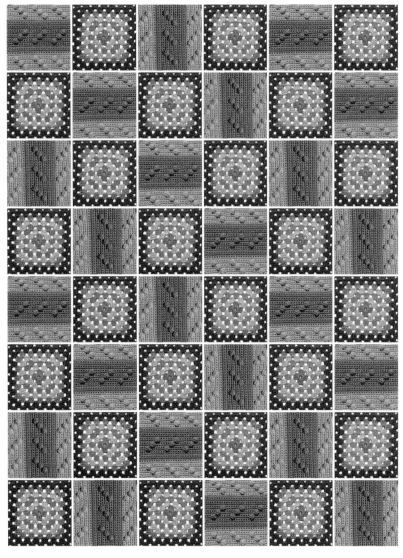

Size:
91cm x 122cm (36" x 48") not including the edging.

Materials:
- 4mm (size F) crochet hook
- DK weight pure wool yarn
  See page 125 for information on how to calculate yarn amounts.

Working the crochet:
Work each of the blocks as described in the Directory and the number of times indicated below.

Finishing:
Sew in all the ends. Block each piece (page 121) and allow to air dry. Lay out the blocks following the pattern (left), stitch or crochet together (page 121) using matching yarn.

Working an edging:
Work two rows of dc edging (page 122) in bronze green yarn around the edge. Alternatively, work a length of Shamrock Edging (page 122) in sage green yarn and stitch it around the edge using matching yarn.

  18 x 24
 Ⓐ Ⓑ Ⓒ
Ⓓ Ⓔ Ⓕ

  203 x 24
Ⓐ Ⓑ Ⓒ

Floral Fantasy

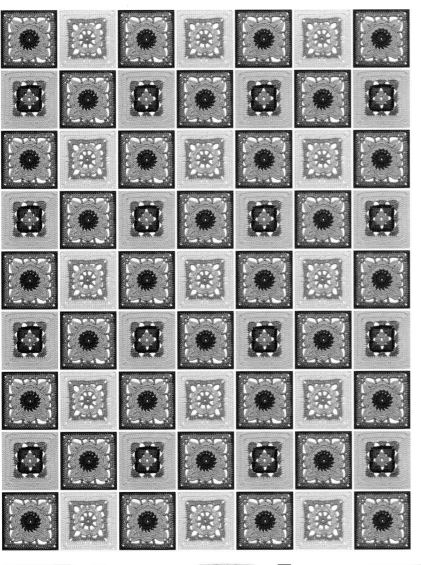

Size:
107cm x 137cm (42" x 54") not including the edging.

Materials:
- 4mm (size F) crochet hook
- DK weight pure wool yarn
  See page 125 for information on how to calculate yarn amounts.

Working the crochet:
Work each of the blocks as described in the Directory and the number of times indicated below.

Finishing:
Sew in all the ends. Block each piece (page 121) and allow to air dry. Lay out the blocks following the pattern (left), stitch or crochet together (page 121) using matching yarn.

Working an edging:
Work a length of Scallop Edging (page 123) in bronze green and stitch it around the edge using matching yarn. Alternatively, work a length of Shell and Lace Edging (page 123) in pale pink and attach in the same way.

 78 x 15
Ⓐ Ⓑ Ⓒ
Ⓓ

 129 x 16
Ⓐ Ⓑ Ⓒ
Ⓓ Ⓔ

 189 x 32
Ⓐ Ⓑ Ⓒ

Merry Xmas

Size:

To fit cushion pad 45cm x 45cm(18" x 18").

Materials:

- 4mm (size F) crochet hook
- DK weight pure wool yarn
  See page 125 for information on how to calculate yarn amounts.

Working the crochet:

Work each of the blocks as described in the Directory and the number of times indicated below.

Finishing:

Sew in all the ends. Block each piece (page 121) and allow to air dry. Lay out the blocks following the pattern (left) to make two identical pieces for front and back of the cushion. Stitch the blocks together (page 121) using matching yarn. Place the front and back pieces together with right sides facing and stitch together around three sides. Turn to the right side, insert the cushion pad and stitch the opening closed.

 25 x 2   A B C   **27** x 8   A B C   **28** x 8   A B C

Fourth of July

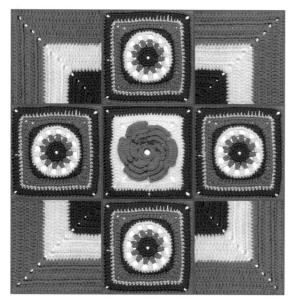

Size:

To fit cushion pad 45cm x 45cm(18" x 18").

Materials:

- 4mm (size F) crochet hook
- DK weight pure wool yarn
  See page 125 for information on how to calculate yarn amounts.

Working the crochet:

Work each of the blocks as described in the Directory and the number of times indicated below.

Finishing:

Sew in all the ends. Block each piece (page 121) and allow to air dry. Lay out the blocks following the pattern (left) to make two identical pieces for front and back of the cushion. Stitch the blocks together (page 121) using matching yarn. Place the front and back pieces together with right sides facing and stitch together around three sides. Turn to the right side, insert the cushion pad and stitch the opening closed.

 65 x 8   A B C   **67** x 2   A B C   **68** x 8   A B C

Baby Stripes

Size:
91cm x 107cm (36" x 42"), without edging.

Materials:
- 4mm (size F) crochet hook
- DK weight pure wool yarn
  See page 125 for information on how to calculate yarn amounts.

Working the crochet:
Work each of the blocks as described in the Directory and the number of times indicated below.

Finishing:
Sew in all the ends. Block each piece (page 121) and allow to air dry. Lay out the blocks following the pattern (right), stitch or crochet together (page 121) using matching yarn.

Working an edging:
Work two rows of dc edging (page 122) in cream yarn around the edge. Finish by working two rows of the same edging in mauve yarn.

 **108** x 42

Pastel Rainbow

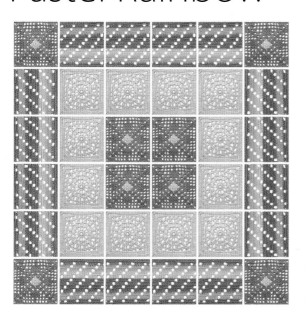

Size:
91cm x 91cm (36" x 36"), without edging.

Materials:
- 4mm (size F) crochet hook
- DK weight pure wool yarn
  See page 125 for information on how to calculate yarn amounts.

Working the crochet:
Work each of the blocks as described in the Directory and the number of times indicated below.

Finishing:
Sew in all the ends. Block each piece (page 121) and allow to air dry. Lay out the blocks following the pattern (left), stitch or crochet together (page 121) using matching yarn.

Working an edging:
To make a simple, narrow edging, work two rows of dc edging (page 122) in sky blue yarn around the edge. Alternatively, work a length of Shamrock Edging (page 122) in sky blue yarn and stitch it around the edge using matching yarn.

 47 x 12

 97 x 16

 100 x 8

Block Directory

The Block Directory contains photographs and patterns for over 200 crochet blocks. Each block is graded by degree of difficulty so you can choose the ones which suit your own skill level. In the last section, each main pattern is shown in the original colour with three different colourways to illustrate the variety of effects you can achieve.

1 Triangle Stripes

11 ⬚
Ⓐ Ⓑ Ⓒ

Special abbreviation

dc3tog = decrease 2 sts by working the next 3 dc together

FOUNDATION CHAIN: Using yarn A, work 2ch.

FOUNDATION ROW: *(wrong side)* Work 3dc into 2nd ch from hook, turn. *(3dc)*

ROW 1: 1ch, 2dc into first dc, 1dc into next dc, 2dc into last dc, turn. *(5dc)* Begin increase pattern.

ROWS 2 to 4: 1ch, 2dc into first dc, 1dc into each dc along row to last st, 2dc into last dc, turn.

ROW 5: 1ch, 1dc into each dc along row, turn.

Rep rows 2 to 5 five times. *(41dc)* Break off yarn A.

Join yarn B and begin decrease pattern.

NEXT ROW: 1ch, 1dc into each dc along row, turn.

NEXT 3 ROWS: 1ch, miss first dc, 1dc into each dc along row to last 2 sts, miss 1 dc, 1dc into last dc, turn. Break off yarn B.

Rep 4-row decrease pattern five times using four-row stripes of colour in the following sequence: C, A, B, C, A. *(5dc)*

NEXT ROW: Continuing with A, 1ch, miss first dc, 1dc into each of next 2dc, miss next dc, 1dc into next dc, turn. *(3dc)*

NEXT ROW: 1ch, work dc3tog. Fasten off yarn.

2 Tiny Textures

1 ⬚
Ⓐ

FOUNDATION CHAIN: Work 32ch.

FOUNDATION ROW: *(right side)* Work 1dc into 2nd ch from hook, 1dc into each chain to end, turn. *(31dc)*

ROW 1: 1ch, 1dc in first dc, *1ch, miss 1dc, 1dc into next dc; rep from * to end, turn.

ROW 2: 1ch, 1dc in first dc, *1tr in next 1ch sp, 1dc into next dc; rep from * to end, turn.

ROW 3: 1ch, 1dc in first dc, *1ch, miss 1dc, 1dc into next dc; rep from * to end, turn.

Rep rows 2 and 3 11 times, ending with a 3rd row.

NEXT ROW: Work 1dc in each st along row.

Fasten off yarn.

MIX-AND-MATCH

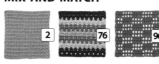

MIX-AND-MATCH

3 Square Target

1 🔄
Ⓐ Ⓑ Ⓒ

4 Bobble Diamond

11 ☰
Ⓐ

FOUNDATION RING: Using yarn A, work 4ch and join with ss to form a ring.

ROUND 1: 5ch *(counts as 1tr, 2ch)*, [3tr into ring, 2ch] 3 times, 2tr into ring, join with ss into 3rd of 5ch. *(four groups of 3tr, four 2ch spaces forming corners)*

ROUND 2: Ss into 2ch sp, 7ch *(counts as 1tr, 4ch)*, * 2tr into same 2ch sp, 1tr into each tr across side of square, ** 2tr into next 2ch sp, 4ch; rep from * twice and from * to ** again, 1tr into last 2ch sp, join with ss to 3rd of 7ch. *(four groups of 7tr, four 4ch spaces forming corners)* Break off yarn A.

ROUND 3: Join yarn B to 4ch sp, 7ch *(counts as 1tr, 4ch)*, * 2tr into same 4ch sp, 1tr into each tr across side of square, ** 2tr into next 4ch sp, 4ch; rep from * twice and from * to ** again, 1tr into last 4ch sp, join with ss to 3rd of 7ch. *(four groups of 11tr, four 4ch spaces forming corners)* Break off yarn B.

ROUND 4: Join yarn C to 4ch sp, rep round 3. *(four groups of 15tr, four 4ch spaces forming corners)* Break off yarn C.

ROUND 5: Join yarn B to 4ch sp, rep round 3. *(four groups of 19tr, four 4ch spaces forming corners)* Break off yarn B.

ROUND 6: Join yarn A to 4ch sp, rep round 3. *(four groups of 23tr, four 4ch spaces forming corners)*

ROUND 7: 1ch, 1dc into each tr in previous round, working [2dc, 1ch, 2dc] into each 4ch corner sp, join with ss into first dc.

ROUND 8: 1ch, 1dc into each dc in previous round, working 2ch at each corner, join with ss into first dc. Fasten off yarn.

MIX-AND-MATCH

 95   **204**   **209**

Special abbreviation

MB = make bobble (work 4 open tr in same st leaving 5 loops on hook, draw yarn through all 5 loops at once)

FOUNDATION CHAIN: Work 28ch.

FOUNDATION ROW: *(wrong side)* Work 1dc into 2nd ch from hook, 1dc into each ch to end, turn. *(27dc)*

ROW 1: 1ch, 1dc into each dc, turn. *(27dc)*

ROWS 2 to 7: Rep row 1.

ROW 8: 1ch, 1dc into each of next 13dc, MB, 1dc into each of next 13dc, turn.

ROWS 9 to 11: Rep row 1.

ROW 12: 1ch, 1dc into each of next 10dc, [MB, 1dc into each of next 2dc] twice, MB, 1dc into each of next 10dc, turn.

ROWS 13 to 15: Rep row 1.

ROW 16: 1ch, 1dc into each of next 7dc, [MB, 1dc into each of next 2dc] 4 times, MB, 1dc into each of next 7dc, turn.

ROWS 17 to 19: Rep row 1.

ROW 20: Rep row 12.

ROWS 21 to 23: Rep row 1.

ROW 24: Rep row 8.

ROWS 25 to 32: Rep row 1.

Fasten off yarn.

MIX-AND-MATCH

 157   **193**   **203**

5 Twin Stripes

1 ≡
Ⓐ Ⓑ Ⓒ
Ⓓ

FOUNDATION CHAIN: Using yarn A, work 32ch.

FOUNDATION ROW: (wrong side) Work 2tr into 5th ch from hook, 2tr into next ch, * miss 2ch, 2tr into each of next 2ch; rep from * to last 2ch, miss1ch, 1tr into last ch, turn.

ROW 1: 3ch (counts as 1tr), * miss 2tr, 2tr into each of next 2 tr; rep from * to last 2 sts, miss 1tr, 1tr into top of turning chain, turn. Break off yarn A. Join yarn B.

Rep row 1 12 times, changing colour in the following sequence:
2 rows in B, 2 rows in C, 2 rows in D, 2 rows in C, 2 rows in B, 2 rows in A.
Fasten off yarn.

6 Textured Bluebells

1 ≡
Ⓐ

FOUNDATION CHAIN: Work 32ch.

FOUNDATION ROW: (right side) Work 1dc into 2nd ch from hook, 1dc into each chain along row, turn. (31dc)

ROW 1: 1ch, * 1dc, 2ch, miss 2 sts; rep from * ending with 1dc, turn.

ROW 2: 3ch (counts as 1tr), 1tr in first dc, then work 3tr in every foll dc until last dc, 2tr in last dc, turn.

ROW 3: 1ch, 1dc in first tr, * 2ch, 1dc into central tr of each group; rep from * ending last rep 2ch, 1dc into 3rd of 3ch, turn.

Rep rows 2 and 3 7 times, then rep row 2 again.

LAST ROW: 1ch, 1dc in each tr along row.
Fasten off yarn.

MIX-AND-MATCH

MIX-AND-MATCH

7 Corner Granny

FOUNDATION RING: Using yarn A, work 6ch and join with ss to form a ring.

ROUND 1: 3ch *(counts as 1tr)*, 2tr into ring, 3ch, * 3tr into ring, 3ch; rep from * twice, join with ss into 3rd of 3ch. Break off yarn A.

ROUND 2: Join yarn B to any 3ch sp, 3ch *(counts as 1tr)*, [2tr, 3ch, 3tr] into same sp to make corner, * 1ch, [3tr, 3ch, 3tr] into next 3ch sp to make corner; rep from * twice, 1ch, join with ss into 3rd of 3ch. Break off yarn B.

ROUND 3: Join yarn C to any 3ch corner sp, 3ch, [2tr, 3ch, 3tr] into same sp, * 1ch, 3tr into next 1ch sp, 1ch, [3tr, 3ch, 3tr] into next 3ch corner sp; rep from * to end, ending with 1ch, join with ss into 3rd of 3ch. Break off yarn C.

ROUND 4: Join yarn D to any 3ch corner sp, 3ch, [2tr ,3ch, 3tr] into same sp, * [1ch, 3tr into each 1ch sp] along side of square, 1ch, [3tr, 3ch, 3tr] into next 3ch corner sp; rep from * to end, 1ch, join with ss into 3rd of 3ch.

ROUND 5: 1ch, 1dc into every tr and 1ch sp of previous round, working [2dc, 1ch, 2dc] into each 3ch corner space, join with ss into first dc. Break off yarn D.

Change from working rounds to working in rows.

ROW 1: Join yarn E to any 1ch corner sp. With RS of square facing and working through back loops of each st on this row only, 1ch, 1dc into each dc along first side of square, 3dc into next 1ch corner sp, 1dc into each dc along next side of square working last dc into corner 1ch sp, turn.

ROW 2: Working through both loops of each st, 1ch, 1dc into each dc of previous row, working 3dc into centre st of 3dc corner group, turn. Rep row 2 nine times, changing yarn colour in the following sequence: 2 more rows in E, 2 rows in C, 2 rows in B, 3 rows in D.

Fasten off yarn.

MIX-AND-MATCH

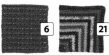

8 Popcorn Flower

Special abbreviations

beg pc = beginning popcorn made from 3ch and 4 tr sts, **pc** = popcorn made from 5 tr sts

FOUNDATION RING: Work 8ch and join with ss to form a ring.

ROUND 1: Beg pc into ring, [5ch, pc into ring] 3 times, 5ch, join with ss into top of beg pc.

ROUND 2: 3ch *(counts as 1tr)*, * [2tr, 2ch, pc, 2ch, 2tr] into next 5ch sp, ** 1tr into next pc; rep from * twice and from * to ** again, join with ss into 3rd of 3ch.

ROUND 3: 3ch *(counts as 1tr)*, 1tr into each of next 2 sts, * 3tr into next 2ch sp, 4ch, 3tr into next 2ch sp, ** 1tr into each tr across side of square; rep from * twice and from * to ** again, 1tr into each of last 2 sts, join with ss into 3rd of 3ch. *(four groups of 11tr, four 4ch spaces forming corners)*

ROUND 4: 3ch *(counts as 1tr)*, 1tr into each of next 5 sts, * [2tr, 4ch, 2tr] into corner sp, ** 1tr into each tr across side of square; rep from * twice and from * to ** again, 1tr into each of last 5 sts, join with ss into 3rd of 3ch. *(four groups of 15tr, four 4ch spaces forming corners)*

ROUND 5: 3ch *(counts as 1tr)*, 1tr into each of next 7 sts, * [2tr, 4ch, 2tr] into corner sp, ** 1tr into each tr across side of square; rep from * twice and from * to ** again, 1tr into each of last 7 sts, join with ss into 3rd of 3ch. *(four groups of 19tr, four 4ch spaces forming corners)*

ROUND 6: 3ch *(counts as 1tr)*, 1tr into each of next 9 sts, * [2tr, 4ch, 2tr] into corner sp, ** 1tr into each tr across side of square; rep from * twice and from * to ** again, 1tr into each of last 9 sts, join with ss into 3rd of 3ch. *(four groups of 23tr, four 4ch spaces forming corners)*

ROUND 7: 1ch, 1dc into each tr in previous round, working [2dc, 1ch, 2dc] into each 4ch corner sp, join with ss into first dc.

ROUND 8: 1ch, 1dc into each dc in previous round, working 2ch at each corner, join with ss into first dc.

Fasten off yarn.

MIX-AND-MATCH

9 Arcadia

FOUNDATION RING: Using yarn A, work 6ch and join with ss to form a ring.

ROUND 1: 3ch *(counts as 1tr)*, 15tr into ring, join with ss into 3rd of 3ch. *(16tr)* Break off yarn A.

ROUND 2: Join yarn B, 5ch *(counts as 1tr, 2ch)*, [1tr into next tr, 2ch] 15 times, join with ss into 3rd of 5ch. *(16 spaced tr)* Break off yarn B.

ROUND 3: Join yarn C to any 2ch sp, 3ch *(counts as 1tr)*, [1tr, 3ch, 2tr] into same sp, * [2ch, 1dc into next 2ch sp] 3 times, 2ch, ** [2tr, 3ch, 2tr] into next 2ch sp; rep from * twice and from * to ** once again, join with ss into 3rd of 3ch.

ROUND 4: Join yarn D to any 3ch corner sp, 3ch *(counts as 1tr)*, [1tr, 3ch, 2tr] into same sp, * [2ch, 1dc into next 2ch sp] 4 times, 2ch, ** [2tr, 3ch, 2tr] into next 3ch corner sp; rep from * twice and from * to ** once again, join with ss into 3rd of 3ch.

ROUND 5: Ss in next tr and into next 3ch sp, 3ch *(counts as 1tr)*, [2tr, 2ch, 3tr] into same sp, * [2ch, 1tr into next 2ch sp] 5 times, 2ch, ** [3tr, 2ch, 3tr] into next 3ch corner sp; rep

from * twice and from * to ** once again, join with ss into 3rd of 3ch.

ROUND 6: Join yarn E to any 2ch corner sp, 3ch *(counts as 1tr)*, [2tr, 2ch, 3tr] into same sp, * [2ch, 1tr into next 2ch sp] 6 times, 2ch, ** [3tr, 2ch, 3tr] into next 2ch corner sp; rep from * twice and from * to ** once again, join with ss into 3rd of 3ch.

ROUND 7: Ss in next 2tr and into next 2ch sp, 3ch *(counts as 1tr)*, [1tr, 2ch, 2tr] into same sp, * 1tr into each tr and 2tr into each 2ch sp along side of square, ** [2tr, 2ch, 2tr] into next 2ch corner sp; rep from * twice and from * to ** once again, join with ss into 3rd of 3ch.

Fasten off yarn.

10 Openwork Square

FOUNDATION CHAIN: Work 34ch.

FOUNDATION ROW: *(right side)* 1dc into 2nd ch from hook, 1dc into each ch, turn. *(33dc)*

ROW 1: 4ch *(counts as 1tr, 1ch)*, miss 1dc, 1tr into next dc, * 1ch, miss 1dc, 1tr into next dc; rep from * to end, turn.

ROW 2: 1ch, 1dc into first tr, 2dc into each 1ch sp along row, ending with 2dc into 1ch sp formed by turning ch, turn. *(33dc)*

ROW 3: 1ch, 1dc into each dc, turn.

Rep rows 1 to 3 7 times.

Fasten off yarn.

MIX-AND-MATCH

MIX-AND-MATCH

11 Baby Blocks

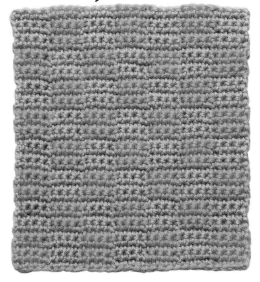

11 ☰
Ⓐ Ⓑ

FOUNDATION CHAIN: Using yarn A, work 29ch.

WORKING THE PATTERN: When following the chart, read odd-numbered rows (right side rows) from right to left and even-numbered rows (wrong side rows) from left to right.

Starting at the bottom right-hand corner of the chart, work the 34 row pattern from the chart in dc. On the first row, work first dc into 2nd ch from hook, 1dc into each ch along row. *(28dc)*

Fasten off yarn.

■ **YARN A**
■ **YARN B**

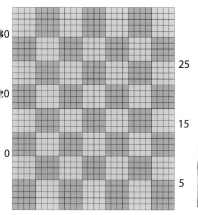

12 Fine Lines

1 ☰
Ⓐ Ⓑ Ⓒ
Ⓓ Ⓔ Ⓕ

FOUNDATION CHAIN: Using yarn A, work 29ch.

FOUNDATION ROW: *(right side)* 1dc into 2nd ch from hook, 1dc into each ch, turn. *(28dc)*

ROW 1: 1ch, 1dc into each dc, turn. *(28dc)*

Rep row 1, working the following colour sequence:

4 more rows in A, 1 row in B, 3 rows in A, 1 row in C, 1 row in A, 1 row in D, 5 rows in A, 1 row in E, 3 rows in A, 1 row in F, 1 row in A, 1 row in C, 3 rows in A, 1 row in B, 6 rows in A.

Fasten off yarn.

MIX-AND-MATCH

MIX-AND-MATCH

13 Circle in a Square

11 📷
Ⓐ Ⓑ Ⓒ
Ⓓ Ⓔ

FOUNDATION RING: Using yarn A, work 8ch and join with ss to form a ring.

ROUND 1: 3ch (counts as 1tr), 15tr into ring, join with ss into 3rd of 3ch. (16tr) Break off yarn A.

ROUND 2: Join yarn B, 5ch (counts as 1tr, 2ch), [1tr into next tr, 2ch] 15 times, join with ss into 3rd of 5ch. (16 spaced tr) Break off yarn B.

ROUND 3: Join yarn C to any 2ch sp, 3ch (counts as 1tr), 2tr into same sp, 1ch, * [3tr, 1ch] into next 2ch sp; rep from * to end, join with ss into 3rd of 3ch. Break off yarn C.

ROUND 4: Join yarn D to any 1ch sp, * [3ch, 1dc into next 1ch sp] 3 times, 6ch to make corner sp, 1dc into next 1ch sp; rep from * to end, join with ss into first of 3ch.

ROUND 5: 3ch (counts as 1tr), 2tr into first 3ch sp, 3tr into each of next two 3ch sps, * [5tr, 2ch, 5tr] into 6ch corner sp, 3tr into each 3ch sp; rep from * to end, join with ss into 3rd of 3ch. Break off yarn D.

ROUND 6: Join yarn E to any tr along side of square, 3ch, work 1tr into each tr of previous round, working [1tr, 1dtr, 1tr] into each 2ch corner sp, join with ss into 3rd of 3ch. Break off yarn E.

ROUND 7: Join yarn A to any tr along side of square, 1ch, 1dc into every tr of previous round, working [1dc, 1ch, 1dc] into each dtr at corner, join with ss into first dc. Break off yarn A.

ROUND 8: Join yarn B, 1ch, 1dc into every dc of previous round, working 3dc into each 1ch corner sp, join with ss into first dc. Fasten off yarn.

MIX-AND-MATCH

14 Alhambra

11 📷 Ⓐ

Special abbreviation
tr2tog = work 2 tr sts together to make cluster

FOUNDATION RING: Work 8ch and join with ss to form a ring.

ROUND 1: 1ch, 16dc into ring, join with ss into first dc. (16dc)

ROUND 2: 1ch, 1dc into same place, [7ch, miss 3dc, 1dc into next dc] 3 times, 7ch, miss 3dc, join with ss into first dc.

ROUND 3: Ss into 3rd ch of next 7ch sp, 3ch (counts as 1tr), 1tr into same place, * 3ch, 2tr into same sp, 3ch, tr2tog inserting hook into same sp for first leg and into next 7ch sp for second leg, 3ch, 2tr into same sp; rep from * 3 times omitting 2tr at end of last rep, join with ss into 3rd of 3ch.

ROUND 4: Ss in next tr and into next 3ch corner sp, 3ch (counts as 1tr), 1tr into same place, * 3ch, 2tr into same 3ch sp, 3ch, miss 2tr, 3tr into next 3ch sp, 1tr into top of next cluster, 3tr into next 3ch sp, 3ch, miss 2tr, 2tr into next 3ch sp; rep from * 3 times, omitting 2tr at end of last rep, join with ss into 3rd of 3ch.

ROUND 5: Ss in next tr and into next 3ch sp, 3ch (counts as 1tr), 2tr into same place, * 3ch, 3tr into same 3ch sp, 2ch, 2tr into next 3ch sp, 2ch, miss 1tr, 1tr into each of next 5tr, 2ch, 2tr into next 3ch sp, 2ch, 3tr into next 3ch sp; rep from * 3 times, omitting 3tr at end of last rep, join with ss into 3rd of 3ch.

ROUND 6: 3ch, 1tr into each of next 2tr, * [3tr, 3ch, 3tr] into next 3ch sp, 1tr into each of next 3tr, 2ch, 2tr into next 2tr, 2ch, miss 1tr, 1tr into each of next 3tr, 2ch, 1tr into each of next 2tr, 2ch, 1tr into each of next 3tr; rep from * 3 times, omitting 3tr at end of last rep, join with ss into 3rd of 3ch.

ROUND 7: 1ch, 1dc into every tr of previous round, working 2dc into every 2ch sp and 5dc into each 3ch corner sp, join with ss into first dc. Fasten off yarn.

MIX-AND-MATCH

15 Corner Square

1 ⊜ Ⓐ Ⓑ Ⓒ Ⓓ Ⓔ Ⓕ

FOUNDATION CHAIN: Using yarn A, work 6ch.

ROW 1: *(right side)* Insert hook into 4th ch from hook, work 3tr, turn.

ROW 2: 3ch *(counts as 1tr)*, 1tr into each of next 2tr, 4tr into loop made by turning ch of previous row, turn.

ROW 3: 3ch *(counts as 1tr)*, 1tr into each of next 2tr, [2tr, 2ch, 2tr] into next tr, 1tr into each of next 2tr, 1tr into 3rd of 3 ch, turn.

ROW 4: 3ch *(counts as 1tr)*, 1tr into each of next 4tr, [2tr, 2ch, 2tr] into 2ch sp, 1tr into each of next 4tr, 1tr into 3rd of 3ch, turn. Break off yarn A.

ROW 5: Join yarn B, 3ch *(counts as 1tr)*, 1tr into each of next 6tr, [2tr, 2ch, 2tr] into 2ch sp, 1tr into each of next 6tr, 1tr into 3rd of 3ch, turn.

ROW 6: 3ch *(counts as 1tr)*, 1tr into each of next 8tr, [2tr, 2ch, 2tr] into 2ch sp, 1tr into each of next 8tr, 1tr into 3rd of 3ch, turn. Break off yarn B.

ROW 7: Join yarn C, 3ch *(counts as 1tr)*, 1tr into each of next 10tr, [2tr, 2ch, 2tr] into 2ch sp, 1tr into each of next 10tr, 1tr into 3rd of 3ch, turn.

ROW 8: 3ch *(counts as 1tr)*, 1tr into each of next 12tr, [2tr, 2ch, 2tr] into 2ch sp, 1tr into each of next 12tr, 1tr into 3rd of 3ch, turn. Break off yarn C.

ROW 9: Join yarn D, 3ch *(counts as 1tr)*, 1tr into each of next 14tr, [2tr, 2ch, 2tr] into 2ch sp, 1tr into each of next 14tr, 1tr into 3rd of 3ch, turn.

ROW 10: 3ch *(counts as 1tr)*, 1tr into each of next 16tr, [2tr, 2ch, 2tr] into 2ch sp, 1tr into each of next 16tr, 1tr into 3rd of 3ch, turn. Break off yarn D.

ROW 11: Join yarn E, 3ch *(counts as 1tr)*, 1tr into each of next 18tr, [2tr, 2ch, 2tr] into 2ch sp, 1tr into each of next 18tr, 1tr into 3rd of 3ch, turn.

ROW 12: 3ch *(counts as 1tr)*, 1tr into each of next 20tr, [2tr, 2ch, 2tr] into 2ch sp, 1tr into each of next 20tr, 1tr into 3rd of 3ch, turn. Break off yarn E.

ROW 13: Join yarn F, 3ch *(counts as 1tr)*, 1tr into each of next 22tr, [2tr, 2ch, 2tr] into 2ch sp, 1tr into each of next 22tr, 1tr into 3rd of 3ch, turn.

ROW 14: 3ch *(counts as 1tr)*, 1tr into each of next 24tr, 5tr into 2ch sp, 1tr into each of next 24tr, 1tr into 3rd of 3ch.

Fasten off yarn.

MIX-AND-MATCH

 34 75 197

16 Waterlily

111 ⌾ Ⓐ Ⓑ Ⓒ

FOUNDATION RING: Using yarn A, work 8ch and join with ss to form a ring.

ROUND 1: 6ch *(counts as 1tr, 3ch)*, [1tr into ring, 3ch] 7 times, join with ss into 3rd of 3ch. *(8 spaced tr)* Break off yarn A.

ROUND 2: Join yarn B to any 3ch sp, [1dc, 2ch, 3tr, 2ch, 1dc] into same sp, * [1dc, 2ch, 3tr, 2ch, 1dc] into next 3ch sp; rep from * 7 times, do not join. *(8 petals)*

ROUND 3: * 5ch, working behind petals, miss 1 petal, 1dc into top of next tr of round 1; rep from * to end, do not join. *(8 5ch loops)*

ROUND 4: * [1dc, 2ch, 5tr, 2ch, 1dc] into next 5ch loop; rep from * to end, do not join. *(8 petals)*

ROUND 5: * 7ch, working behind petals, miss 1 petal, 1dc into next dc of round 3; rep from * to end, do not join. *(8 7ch loops)*

ROUND 6: * [1dc, 2ch, 7tr, 2ch, 1dc] into next 7ch loop; rep from * to end, join with ss into first dc. *(8 petals)* Break off yarn B.

ROUND 7: Working behind petals, join yarn C to any dc on round 5,

3ch *(counts as 1tr)*, 2tr into same dc, 3ch, * [3tr, 3ch, 3tr] into next dc of round 5 to make corner, 3ch, ** 3tr into next dc, 3ch; rep from * twice and from * to ** once again, join with ss into 3rd of 3ch.

ROUND 8: 3ch *(counts as 1tr)*, 1tr into every tr and 3tr into each 3ch sp of previous round, working [2tr, 3ch, 2tr] into each 3ch corner sp, join with ss into 3rd of 3ch.

ROUND 9: 3ch *(counts as 1tr)*, 1tr into each tr of previous round, working [2tr, 3ch, 2tr] into each 3ch corner sp, join with ss into 3rd of 3ch.

ROUND 10: 1ch, 1dc into each tr of previous round, working [2dc, 1ch, 2dc] into each 3ch corner sp, join with ss into first dc. Break off yarn C.

ROUND 11: Join yarn B, 1ch, 1dc into each dc of previous round, working 3dc into each 1ch corner sp, join with ss into first dc.

Fasten off yarn.

MIX-AND-MATCH

 43 44 167

17 Alternate Bobbles

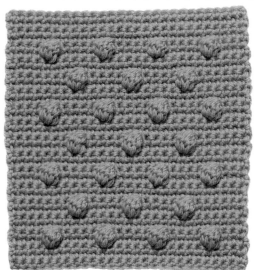

11

Ⓐ

Special abbreviation

MB = make bobble (work 4 open tr in same st leaving 5 loops on hook, draw yarn through all 5 loops at once)

FOUNDATION CHAIN: Work 28ch.

FOUNDATION ROW: *(wrong side)*
Working first dc into 2nd ch from hook, work 1dc into each ch, turn. *(27dc)*

ROW 1: 1ch, 1dc into each dc, turn. *(27dc)*

ROWS 2 & 3: Rep row 1.

ROW 4: 1ch, 1dc into each of next 4dc, [MB, 1dc into each of next 5dc] 3 times, MB, 1dc into each of next 4dc, turn.

ROWS 5 to 7: Rep row 1.

ROW 8: 1ch, 1dc into each of next 7dc, [MB, 1dc into each of next 5dc] twice, MB, 1dc into each of next 7dc, turn.

Rep rows 1 to 8 twice, then rep rows 1 to 7 once again.

NEXT ROW: Rep row 1.
Fasten off yarn.

MIX-AND-MATCH

18 Traditional Granny

1 Ⓐ Ⓑ Ⓒ Ⓓ Ⓔ Ⓕ

FOUNDATION RING: Using yarn A, work 6ch and join with ss to form a ring.

ROUND 1: 3ch *(counts as 1tr)*, 2tr into ring, 3ch, * 3tr into ring, 3ch; rep from * twice more, join with ss into 3rd of 3ch. Break off yarn A.

ROUND 2: Join yarn B to any 3ch sp, 3ch *(counts as 1tr)*, [2tr, 3ch, 3tr] into same sp *(corner made)*, * 1ch, [3tr, 3ch, 3tr] into next 3ch sp; rep from * twice more, 1ch, join with ss into 3rd of 3ch. Break off yarn B.

ROUND 3: Join yarn C to any 3ch corner sp, 3ch *(counts as 1tr)*, [2tr, 3ch, 3tr] into same sp, * 1ch, 3tr into 1ch sp, 1ch, ** [3tr, 3ch, 3tr] into next 3ch corner sp; rep from * twice and from * to ** once again, join with ss into 3rd of 3ch. Break off yarn C.

ROUND 4: Join yarn D to any 3ch corner sp, 3ch *(counts as 1tr)*, [2tr, 3ch, 3tr] into same sp, * [1ch, 3tr] into each 1ch sp along side of square, 1ch, ** [3tr, 3ch, 3tr] into next 3ch corner sp; rep from * twice and from * to ** once again, join with ss into 3rd of 3ch. Break off yarn D.

ROUND 5: Join yarn E to any 3ch corner sp, 3ch *(counts as 1tr)*, [2tr, 3ch, 3tr] into same sp, * [1ch, 3tr] into each 1ch sp along side of square, 1ch, ** [3tr, 3ch, 3tr] into next 3ch corner sp; rep from * twice and from * to ** once again, join with ss into 3rd of 3ch. Break off yarn E.

ROUND 6: Join yarn F to any 3ch corner sp, 3ch *(counts as 1tr)*, [2tr, 3ch, 3tr] into same sp, * [1ch, 3tr] into each 1ch sp along side of square, 1ch, ** [3tr, 3ch, 3tr] into next 3ch corner sp; rep from * twice and from * to ** once again, join with ss into 3rd of 3ch.

ROUND 7: Ss in next 2tr and into next 3ch corner sp, 3ch *(counts as 1tr)*, [2tr, 3ch, 3tr] into same sp, * [1ch, 3tr] into each 1ch sp along side of square, 1ch, ** [3tr, 3ch, 3tr] into next 3ch corner sp; rep from * twice and from * to ** once again, join with ss into 3rd of 3ch.
Fasten off yarn.

MIX-AND-MATCH

19 Lacy Cross

1 **A**

FOUNDATION RING: Work 6ch and join with ss to form a ring.

ROUND 1: 3ch *(counts as 1tr)*, 15tr into ring, join with ss into 3rd of 3ch.

ROUND 2: 3ch *(counts as 1tr)*, 2tr into same place, 2ch, miss 1tr, 1tr into next tr, 2ch, miss 1tr, *3tr into next tr, 2ch, miss 1tr, 1tr into next tr, 2ch, miss 1tr; rep from * twice, join with ss into 3rd of 3ch.

ROUND 3: 3ch *(counts as 1tr)*, 5tr into next tr, * 1tr into next tr, [2ch, 1tr into next tr] twice, 5tr into next tr; rep from * twice, [1tr into next tr, 2ch] twice, join with ss into 3rd of 3ch.

ROUND 4: 3ch *(counts as 1tr)*, 1tr into each of next 2tr, 5tr into next tr, * 1tr into each of next 3tr, 2ch, 1tr into next tr, 2ch, 1tr into each of next 3tr, 5tr into next tr; rep from * twice, 1tr into each of next 3tr, 2ch, 1tr into next tr, 2ch, join with ss into 3rd of 3ch.

ROUND 5: 3ch *(counts as 1tr)*, 1tr into each of next 4tr, 5tr into next tr, * 1tr into each of next 5tr, 2ch, 1tr into next tr, 2ch, 1tr into each of next 5tr, 5tr into next tr; rep from * twice, 1tr into each of next 5tr, 2ch, 1tr into next tr, 2ch, join with ss into 3rd of 3ch.

ROUND 6: 3ch *(counts as 1tr)*, 1tr into each of next 6tr, 5tr into next tr, * 1tr into each of next 7tr, 2ch, 1tr into next tr, 2ch, 1tr into each of next 7tr, 5tr into next tr; rep from * twice, 1tr into each of next 7tr, 2ch, 1tr into next tr, 2ch, join with ss into 3rd of 3ch.

ROUND 7: 3ch *(counts as 1tr)*, work 1tr into each tr and 2tr into each 2ch sp of previous round, working [2tr, 1ch, 2tr] into centre st of each 5tr corner group, join with ss into 3rd of 3ch. Fasten off yarn.

MIX-AND-MATCH

 137   **158** **162**

20 Colourful Bobbles

111  **A B C D E F**

Special abbreviation

MB = make bobble (work 4 open tr in same st leaving 5 loops on hook, draw yarn through all 5 loops at once)

FOUNDATION CHAIN: Using yarn A, work 28ch.

FOUNDATION ROW: *(wrong side)* Working first dc into 2nd ch from hook, work 1dc into each ch, turn. *(27dc)*

ROW 1: 1ch, 1dc into each dc, turn.

ROWS 2 & 3: Rep row 1.

ROW 4: 1ch, 1dc into each of next 3dc, MB in B, 1dc into each of next 4dc, MB in C, 1dc into each of next 4dc, MB in D, 1dc into each of next 4dc, MB in E, 1dc into each of next 4dc, MB in F, 1dc into each of next 3dc, turn.

ROWS 5 to 11: Rep row 1.

ROW 12: 1ch, 1dc into each of next 3dc, MB in D, 1dc into each of next 4dc, MB in F, 1dc into each of next 4dc, MB in E, 1dc into each of next 4dc, MB in B, 1dc into each of next 4dc, MB in C, 1dc into each of next 3dc, turn.

ROWS 13 to 19: Rep row 1.

ROW 20: 1ch, 1dc into each of next 3dc, MB in E, 1dc into each of next 4dc, MB in B, 1dc into each of next 4dc, MB in C, 1dc into each of next 4dc, MB in F, 1dc into each of next 4dc, MB in D, 1dc into each of next 3dc, turn.

ROWS 21 to 27: Work in dc across row, 1ch, turn.

ROW 28: 1ch, 1dc into each of next 3dc, MB in C, 1dc into each of next 4dc, MB in D, 1dc into each of next 4dc, MB in F, 1dc into each of next 4dc, MB in B, 1dc into each of next 4dc, MB in E, 1dc into each of next 3dc, turn.

ROWS 29 to 32: Rep row 1. Fasten off yarn.

MIX-AND-MATCH

 127   **131**   **175**

21 Blue Shades

Special abbreviation

dc3tog = decrease 2 sts by working the next 3 dc together

FOUNDATION CHAIN: Using yarn A, work 58ch.

FOUNDATION ROW: *(wrong side)* 1dc into 2nd ch from hook, 1dc into each ch, turn. *(57dc)*

ROW 1: 1ch, 1dc into each of next 27dc, dc3tog, 1dc into each of rem 27dc, turn. *(55dc)*

ROW 2: 1ch, 1dc into each of next 26dc, dc3tog, 1dc into each of rem 26dc, turn. *(53dc)* Break off yarn A.

ROW 3: Join yarn B, 1ch, 1dc into each of next 25dc, dc3tog, 1dc into each of rem 25dc, turn. *(51dc)*

ROW 4: 1ch, 1dc into each of next 24dc, dc3tog, 1dc into each of rem 24dc, turn. *(49dc)* Break off yarn B.

Join yarn C. Cont in pattern as set, working dc3tog over 3 centre sts on every row. At the same time, change yarn colours in the

following colour sequence: Work 2 rows in yarn C, 2 rows in yarn D, 2 rows in yarn E, 2 rows in yarn F, 2 rows in yarn G, 2 rows in yarn F, 2 rows in yarn E, 2 rows in yarn D, 2 rows in yarn C, 2 rows in yarn B.

Join yarn A and cont in pattern until 3dc rem.

NEXT ROW: Work dc3tog.

Fasten off yarn.

MIX-AND-MATCH

22 St Petersburg

Special abbreviations

fptr = front post treble crochet,
bptr = back post treble crochet

FOUNDATION RING: Using yarn A, work 8ch and join with ss to form a ring.

ROUND 1: 6ch *(counts as 1tr, 3ch)*, [3tr into ring, 3ch] 3 times, 2tr into ring, join with ss into 3rd of 6ch. Break off yarn A.

ROUND 2: Join yarn B to any 3ch corner sp, 3ch *(counts as 1tr)*, 2tr into same sp, * 1fptr round each of next 3tr, ** [3tr, 3ch, 3tr] into next 3ch corner sp; rep from * twice and from * to ** once again, [3tr, 3ch] into next 3ch corner sp, join with ss into 3rd of 3ch. Break off yarn B.

ROUND 3: Join yarn C to any 3ch corner sp, 6ch *(counts as 1tr, 3ch)*, 3tr into same sp, * 1bptr round each of next 3sts, 1fptr round each of next 3sts, 1bptr round each of next 3sts, ** [3tr, 3ch, 3tr] into next 3ch corner sp; rep from * twice and from * to ** once again, 2tr into next 3ch corner sp, join with ss into 3rd of 6ch. Break off yarn C.

ROUND 4: Join yarn B to any 3ch corner sp, 3ch *(counts as 1tr)*, 2tr into same sp, * [1fptr round each of next 3sts, 1bptr round each of next 3sts] twice, 1fptr round each of next 3sts, ** [3tr, 3ch, 3tr] into next 3ch corner sp; rep from * twice and from * to ** once again, [3tr, 3ch] into next 3ch corner sp, join with ss into 3rd of 3ch. Break off yarn B.

ROUND 5: Join yarn A to any 3ch corner sp, 1ch, [2dc, 1ch, 2dc] into same sp, * 1dc into each of next 3tr, 1htr into each of next 15tr, 1dc into each of next 3tr, ** [2dc, 1ch, 2dc] into next 3ch corner sp; rep from * twice and from * to ** once again, join with ss into first dc. Break off yarn A.

ROUND 6: Join yarn C to any 1ch corner sp, 2ch *(counts as 1htr)*, 2htr into same sp, * 1htr into each of next 5dc, 1tr into each of next 15htr, 1htr into each of next 5dc, ** 3htr into next 1ch corner sp; rep from * twice and from * to ** once again, join with ss into 2nd of 2ch. Break off yarn C.

ROUND 7: Join yarn A to any tr, 1ch, 1dc into each htr and tr of previous round, working 3dc into centre st of 3htr corner group, join with ss into first dc.

Fasten off yarn.

MIX-AND-MATCH

23 Bars & Diamonds

11 ≡
A

FOUNDATION CHAIN: Work 34ch.

FOUNDATION ROW: *(wrong side)* 1dc into 2nd ch from hook, 1dc into each ch, turn. *(33dc)*

ROW 1: 3ch *(counts as 1tr)*, 1tr into next dc, * miss 2dc, 1tr into next dc, 3ch, work block of 3 evenly spaced tr into side of tr just made, miss 2dc, 1tr into each of next 3dc; rep from * ending last rep with 2tr, turn.

ROW 2: 3ch *(counts as 1tr)*, 1tr into next tr, * 2ch, 1dc into 3rd of 3ch at top corner of next block, 2ch, 1tr into each of next 3tr; rep from * ending last rep with 2tr, turn.

ROW 3: 3ch *(counts as 1tr)*, 1tr into next tr, * 1tr into next dc, 3ch, work block of 3 evenly spaced tr into side of tr just made, 1tr into each of next 3tr; rep from * ending last rep with 2tr, turn.

Rep rows 2 and 3 5 times, then rep row 2 once again.

NEXT ROW: 1ch, 1dc into each of next 2tr, * 2dc into next 2ch sp, 1dc into next dc, 2dc into next 2ch sp, 1dc into each of next 3tr; rep from * ending last rep with 2dc.

Fasten off yarn.

MIX-AND-MATCH

 56 82 105

24 Italian Cross

11 📷 A B C

Special abbreviations

beg pf = beginning puff st of htr3tog, **pf** = puff stitch of htr4tog

FOUNDATION RING: Using yarn A, work 4ch and join with ss to form a ring.

ROUND 1: 3ch *(counts as 1tr)*, 11tr into ring, join with ss into 3rd of 3ch. *(12tr)* Break off yarn A.

ROUND 2: Join yarn B, 2ch *(counts as 1htr)*, beg pf in same place, * [1ch, pf into next st] twice, 5ch, ** pf into next st; rep from * twice and from * to ** once again, join with ss into top of beg pf.

ROUND 3: Ss into next 1ch sp, 2ch *(counts as 1htr)*, beg pf into same sp, * 1ch, pf into next sp, 2ch, 5tr into next 5ch sp, 2ch, ** pf into next 1ch sp; rep from * twice and from * to ** once again, join with ss into top of beg pf.

ROUND 4: Ss into next 1ch sp, 2ch *(counts as 1htr)*, beg pf into same sp, * 3ch, miss 2ch, [1tr into next tr, 1ch] twice, [1tr, 1ch, 1tr, 1ch, 1tr] into next tr, [1ch, 1tr into next tr] twice, 3ch, miss 2ch, ** pf into next 1ch sp; rep from * twice and from * to ** once again, join with ss into top of beg pf. Break off yarn B.

ROUND 5: Join yarn C to first tr of any 7tr corner group, 4ch *(counts as 1tr, 1ch)*, * [1tr into next tr, 1ch] twice, [1tr, 1ch, 1tr, 1ch, 1tr] into next tr, [1ch, 1tr into next tr] 3 times, 3tr into next 3ch sp, 1ch, 3tr into next 3ch sp, ** 1tr into next tr, 1ch; rep from * twice and from * to ** once again, join with ss into 3rd of 4ch.

ROUND 6: 4ch *(counts as 1tr, 1ch)*, * [1tr into next tr, 1ch] 3 times, [1tr, 1ch, 1tr, 1ch, 1tr] into next tr, [1ch, 1tr into next tr] 4 times, 1tr into each of next 3tr, 1tr into 1ch sp, 1tr into each of next 3tr, ** 1tr into next tr, 1ch; rep from * twice and from * to ** once again, join with ss into 3rd of 4ch.

ROUND 7: 4ch *(counts as 1tr, 1ch)*, * [1tr into next tr, 1ch] 4 times, [1tr, 1ch, 1tr, 1ch, 1tr] into next tr, [1ch, 1tr into next tr] 5 times, **1tr into each of next 8tr, 1ch; rep from * twice and from * to ** once again, 1tr into each of next 7tr, join with ss into 3rd of 4ch.

Fasten off yarn.

MIX-AND-MATCH

 47 81 84

25 Tannenbaum

11 ≡
A B C

FOUNDATION CHAIN: Using yarn A, work 29ch.

WORKING THE PATTERN: When following the chart, read odd-numbered rows (right side rows) from right to left and even-numbered rows (wrong side rows) from left to right.

Starting at the bottom right-hand corner of the chart, work the 34 row pattern from the chart in dc. On the first row, work first dc into 2nd ch from hook, 1dc into each ch along row. *(28dc)*

Fasten off yarn.

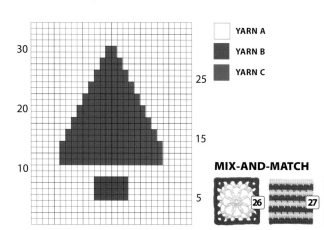

	YARN A
	YARN B
	YARN C

MIX-AND-MATCH

26 Snowflake

11 ⊙ A B

Special abbreviations

beg cl = beginning cluster made from 3 tr stitches, **cl** = cluster made from 4 tr stitches

FOUNDATION RING: Using yarn A, work 8ch and join with ss to form a ring.

ROUND 1: 3ch *(counts as 1tr)*, 2tr into ring, 7ch, [3tr, 7ch] 7 times into ring, join with ss into 3rd of 3ch.

ROUND 2: Ss across next 2tr and 2ch, 3ch *(counts as 1tr)*, beg cl into first 7ch sp, * 9ch, cl into next 7ch sp; rep from * 6 times, 9ch, join with ss into top of beg cl.

ROUND 3: 1ch, * [2dc, 5ch, 2dc] into next 9ch sp, 7ch, [cl, 5ch, cl] into next 9ch sp, 7ch; rep from * 3 times, join with ss into first dc.

Break off yarn A.

ROUND 4: Join yarn B to 5ch sp between 2 groups of 2dc, 2dc into same loop, * 5ch, 2dc into next 7ch sp, 5ch, [cl, 5ch, cl] into next 5ch sp, 5ch, 2dc into 7 ch sp, 5ch, ** 2dc into next 5ch sp; rep from * twice and from * to ** once again, join with ss into first dc.

ROUND 5: 2ch *(counts as 1htr)*, 1htr into next dc, 3dc into next 5ch sp, 1htr into each of next 2dc, 3dc into next 5ch sp, * 1dc into top of next cl, [1dc, 1htr, 1tr, 1htr, 1dc] into next 5ch corner sp, 1dc into next cl, ** [3dc into next 5ch sp, 1htr into each of next 2dc] 3 times, 3dc into next 5ch sp; rep from * twice and from * to ** once again, 3dc into next 5ch sp, 1htr into each of next 2dc, 3dc into next 5ch sp, join with ss into 2nd of 2ch.

ROUND 6: 1ch, 1dc into each dc and htr of previous round, working 5dc into centre st of each corner group.

Fasten off yarn.

MIX-AND-MATCH

Snowy Stripes

11 ≋
Ⓐ Ⓑ Ⓒ

Special abbreviation

sp = spike (insert hook 1 row below next st, pull up loop of yarn, insert hook into top of next st, yo, draw loop through, yo, draw through all 3 loops on hook)

FOUNDATION CHAIN: Using yarn A, work 30ch.

FOUNDATION ROW: *(right side)* 1dc into 2nd ch from hook, 1dc into each ch to end, turn. *(29dc)*

ROW 1: 1ch, 1dc into each st of previous row, turn. *(29dc)*

ROWS 2 & 3: Rep row 1. Break off yarn A.

ROW 4: Join yarn B, 1ch, 1dc into each of next 2dc, * sp into next st, 1dc into each of next 3dc; rep from * to last 2 sts, 1dc into each of next 2dc, turn.

ROWS 5 to 7: Rep row 1. Break off yarn B.

ROW 8: Join yarn C, 1ch, 1dc into each of next 4dc, * sp into next st,

1dc into each of next 3dc; rep from * to last 4 sts, 1dc into each of next 4dc, turn.

ROWS 9 to 11: Rep row 1. Break off yarn C.

ROW 12: Join yarn B, rep row 4.

ROWS 13 to 15: Rep row 1. Break off yarn B.

ROW 16: Join yarn A, rep row 8. Rep rows 1 to 15 once again. Fasten off yarn.

MIX-AND-MATCH

 25   26   28

Christmas Rose

111 📷 Ⓐ Ⓑ Ⓒ

FOUNDATION RING: Using yarn A, work 12ch and join with ss to form a ring.

ROUND 1: 1ch, 18dc into ring, join with ss into first dc.

ROUND 2: 1ch, 1dc into same place, [3ch, miss 2dc, 1dc into next dc] 5 times, 3ch, miss 2dc, join with ss into first dc. *(6 3ch loops)*

ROUND 3: 1ch, [1dc, 3ch, 5tr, 3ch, 1dc] into each of next 6 3ch loops, join with ss into first dc. *(6 petals)*

ROUND 4: 1ch, 1dc into same place, [5ch behind petal of previous round, 1dc between 2dc] 5 times, 5ch behind petal of previous round, join with ss into first dc. *(6 5ch loops)*

ROUND 5: 1ch, [1dc, 3ch, 7tr, 3ch, 1dc] into each of next 6 5ch loops, join with ss into first dc. *(6 petals)* Break off yarn A.

ROUND 6: Join yarn B between any 2dc, 1ch, [1dc between 2dc, 6ch behind petal of previous round] 6 times, join with ss into first dc. *(6 6ch loops)*

ROUND 7: Ss into next 6ch loop, 3ch *(counts as 1tr)*, [4tr, 2ch, 1tr] into same loop, * 6tr into next 6ch loop, [2tr,

2ch, 4tr] into next 6ch loop, ** [5tr, 2ch, 1tr] into next 6ch loop; rep from * to ** once, join with ss into 3rd of 3ch. *(9tr along each side of square)*

ROUND 8: 3ch *(counts as 1tr)*, 1tr into each tr of previous round, working [3tr, 2ch, 3tr] into each 2ch corner sp, join with ss into 3rd of 3ch.

ROUND 9: 3ch *(counts as 1tr)*, 1tr into each tr of previous round, working [2tr, 1dtr, 2ch, 1dtr, 2tr] into each 2ch corner sp, join with ss into 3rd of 3ch. Break off yarn B.

ROUND 10: Join yarn A to any tr of previous round, 1ch, 1dc into each tr and dtr of previous round, working [2dc, 2ch, 2dc] into each 2ch corner sp, join with ss into first dc. Break off yarn A.

ROUND 11: Join yarn C, 1ch, 1dc into each dc of previous round, working 3dc into each 2ch corner sp, join with ss into first dc.

ROUNDS 12 & 13: 1ch, 1dc into each dc of previous round, working 3dc into centre st of each 3dc corner group, join with ss into first dc. Fasten off yarn.

MIX-AND-MATCH

 25   26   27

29 Bobble Stripes

11

Special abbreviation

MB = make bobble (work 4 open tr in same st leaving 5 loops on hook, draw yarn through all 5 loops at once)

FOUNDATION CHAIN: Using yarn A, work 28ch.

FOUNDATION ROW: *(wrong side)* Working first dc into 2nd ch from hook, work 1dc into each ch, turn. *(27dc)*

ROW 1: 1ch, 1dc into each dc, turn.

ROWS 2 & 3: Rep row 1. Break yarn A.

ROW 4: Join yarn B, 1ch, 1dc into next dc, * MB, 1dc into each of next 5dc; rep from * 3 times, MB, 1dc into next dc, turn. Break off yarn B.

ROW 5: Join yarn A and rep row 1.

ROWS 6 to 9: Rep row 1. Break off yarn A.

ROW 10: Join yarn C, 1ch, 1dc into next dc, * MB, 1dc into each of next 5dc; rep from * 3 times, MB, 1dc into next dc, turn. Break off yarn C.

ROW 11: Join yarn A and rep row 1.

ROWS 12 to 15: Rep row 1. Break off yarn A.

ROW 16: Join yarn D, 1ch, 1dc into next dc, * MB, 1dc into each of next 5dc; rep from * 3 times, MB, 1dc into next dc, turn. Break off yarn D.

ROW 17: Join yarn A and rep row 1.

ROWS 18 to 21: Rep row 1. Break off yarn A.

ROW 22: Join yarn E, 1ch, 1dc into next dc, * MB, 1dc into each of next 5dc; rep from * 3 times, MB, 1dc into next dc, turn. Break off yarn E.

ROW 23: Join yarn A and rep row 1.

ROWS 24 to 27: Rep row 1. Break off yarn A.

ROW 28: Join yarn F, 1ch, 1dc into next dc, * MB, 1dc into each of next 5dc; rep from * 3 times, MB, 1dc into next dc, turn. Break off yarn F.

ROW 29: Join yarn A and rep row 1.

ROWS 30 to 32: Rep row 1. Fasten off yarn.

MIX-AND-MATCH

30 Shell Lace

11

FOUNDATION CHAIN: Work 32ch.

FOUNDATION ROW: *(wrong side)* 1dc into 2nd ch from hook, 1dc into next ch, * 3ch, miss 3ch, 1dc into each of next 3ch; rep from * to last 5ch, 3ch, miss 3ch, 1dc into each of last 2ch, turn.

ROW 1: *(right side)* 1ch, 1dc into first dc, * 5tr into 3ch sp, miss 1dc, 1dc into next dc; rep from * to end, turn.

ROW 2: 3ch, 1dc into 2nd, 3rd and 4th stitches of 5tr group, 3ch; rep from * to end, ending with 1dc into 2nd, 3rd and 4th stitch of 5tr group, 2ch, 1dc into last st, turn.

ROW 3: 3ch, 2tr into 2ch sp, miss 1dc, 1dc into next dc, * 5tr into 3ch sp, miss 1dc, 1dc into next dc; rep from * to end, 3tr into last 3ch sp, turn.

ROW 4: 1ch, 1dc into each of first 2tr, * 3ch, 1dc into 2nd, 3rd and 4th stitches of 5tr group; rep from * to end, ending with 3ch, 1dc into 2nd tr, 1dc into 3rd of 3ch, turn.

Rep rows 1 to 4 four times, ending with a 4th row.

Fasten off yarn

MIX-AND-MATCH

31 Primrose Square

 A B C D

Special abbreviations

beg cl = beginning cluster made from 3 tr sts, **cl** = cluster made from 4 tr sts

FOUNDATION RING: Using yarn A, work 6ch and join with ss to form a ring.

ROUND 1: 5ch *(counts as 1tr, 2ch)*, [1tr into ring, 2ch] 7 times, join with ss into 3rd of 5ch. *(8 spaced tr)*

ROUND 2: 3ch *(counts as 1tr)*, beg cl into next 2ch sp, [5ch, cl into next 2ch sp] 7 times, 5ch, join with ss into top of beg cl. Break off yarn A.

ROUND 3: Join yarn B, 1ch, 1dc into same place, * 2ch, working over 5ch sp to enclose it work 1tr into next tr of round 1, 2ch, 1dc into top of next cl; rep from * to end omitting last dc, join with ss into first dc.

ROUND 4: Ss into next ch, 1ch, 1dc into same place, * 3ch, 1dc into next 2ch sp; rep from * to end omitting last dc, join with ss into first dc.

ROUND 5: Ss into next ch, 3ch *(counts as 1tr)*, [1tr, 2ch, 2tr] into same sp, * 2ch, 1dc into next 3ch sp, [3ch, 1dc into next 3ch sp] twice, 2ch, ** [2tr, 2ch 2tr] into next 3ch sp; rep from * twice and from * to ** once again, join with ss into 3rd of 3ch. Break off yarn B.

ROUND 6: Join yarn C into any 2ch corner sp, 3ch *(counts as 1tr)*, [1tr, 2ch, 2tr] into same sp, * 2ch [1dc into next ch sp, 3ch] 3 times, 1dc into next ch sp, 2ch, ** [2tr, 2ch, 2tr] into 2ch corner sp; rep from * twice and from * to ** once again, join with ss into 3rd of 3ch.

ROUND 7: Ss into next 2ch corner sp, 3ch *(counts as 1tr)*, [1tr, 2ch, 2tr] into same sp, * 2ch [1dc into next ch sp, 3ch] 4 times, 1dc into next ch sp, 2ch, ** [2tr, 2ch, 2tr] into 2ch corner sp; rep from * twice and from * to ** once again, join with ss into 3rd of 3ch.

ROUND 8: Ss into next 2ch corner sp, 3ch *(counts as 1tr)*, [1tr, 2ch, 2tr] into same sp, * 2ch [1dc into next ch sp, 3ch] 5 times, 1dc into next ch sp, 2ch, ** [2tr, 2ch, 2tr] into 2ch corner sp; rep from * twice and from * to ** once again, join with ss into 3rd of 3ch.

ROUND 9: Ss into next 2ch corner sp, 3ch *(counts as 1tr)*, [2tr, 2ch, 3tr] into same sp, * 3tr into each ch sp along side of square, ** [3tr, 2ch, 3tr] into next 2ch corner sp; rep from * twice and from * to ** once again, join with ss into 3rd of 3ch. Break off yarn C.

ROUND 10: Join yarn D into any tr along side of square, 1ch, 1dc into same place, 1dc into each tr of previous round, working 3dc into each 2ch corner sp, join with ss into first dc. Fasten off yarn.

MIX-AND-MATCH

 137 157 161

32 Oblique Stripe

11 ☰
A B

Special abbreviation

dc3tog = decrease 2 sts by working the next 3 dc together

FOUNDATION CHAIN: Using yarn A, work 2ch.

FOUNDATION ROW: *(wrong side)* Work 3dc into 2nd ch from hook, turn. *(3dc)*

ROW 1: 1ch, 2dc into first dc, 1dc into next dc, 2dc into last dc, turn. *(5dc)* Begin increase pattern.

ROWS 2 to 4: 1ch, 2dc into first dc, 1dc into each dc along row to last st, 2dc into last st, turn.

ROW 5: 1ch, 1dc into each dc along row, turn.

Rep rows 2 to 5 three times. *(29dc)* Break off yarn A.

Join yarn B, rep rows 3 to 6 twice. *(41dc)* Break off yarn B.

Join yarn A and begin decrease pattern.

NEXT ROW: 1ch, 1dc into each dc along row, turn.

NEXT 3 ROWS: 1ch, miss first dc, 1dc into each dc along row to last 2 sts, miss 1dc, 1dc into last dc, turn. Rep four-row decrease pattern five times. *(5dc)*

NEXT ROW: 1ch, miss first dc, 1dc into each of next 2dc, miss next dc, 1dc into next dc, turn. *(3dc)*

NEXT ROW: 1ch, work dc3tog. Fasten off yarn.

MIX-AND-MATCH

 29 55 156

33 Pretty in Pink

11

Special abbreviation

dc3tog = decrease 2 sts by working the next 3 dc together

FOUNDATION CHAIN: Using yarn A, work 58ch.

FOUNDATION ROW: *(wrong side)* 1dc into 2nd ch from hook, 1dc into each ch, turn. *(57dc)*

ROW 1: 1ch, 1dc into each of next 27dc, dc3tog, 1dc into each of rem 27dc, turn. *(55dc)*

ROW 2: 1ch, 1dc into each of next 26dc, dc3tog, 1dc into each of rem 26dc, turn. *(53dc)*

ROW 3: 1ch, 1dc into each of next 25dc, dc3tog, 1dc into each of rem 25dc, turn. *(51dc)*

ROW 4: 1ch, 1dc into each of next 24dc, dc3tog, 1dc into each of rem 24dc, turn. *(49dc)*

Cont in pattern as set, working dc3tog over 3 centre sts on every row. At the same time, change yarn colours in the following colour sequence:

Work 10 more rows in yarn A, 2 rows in yarn B, 2 rows in yarn C, 2 rows in yarn D, 2 rows in yarn E, 2 rows in yarn F.

Join yarn A and cont in pattern until 3dc rem.

NEXT ROW: Work dc3tog.

Fasten off yarn.

MIX-AND-MATCH

34 Band of Bobbles

11

Special abbreviation

MB = make bobble (work 4 open tr in same st leaving 5 loops on hook, draw yarn through all 5 loops at once)

FOUNDATION CHAIN: Work 28ch.

FOUNDATION ROW: *(wrong side)* Working first dc into 2nd ch from hook, work 1dc into each ch, turn. *(27dc)*

ROW 1: 1ch, 1dc into each dc, turn. *(27dc)*

ROW 2: 1ch, 1dc into first dc, [MB, 1dc into each of next 2dc] 8 times, MB, 1dc into last dc, turn.

ROWS 3 & 4: Rep row 1.

Rep rows 1 to 4 three times, then rep row 1 16 times.

Fasten off yarn.

MIX-AND-MATCH

35 Tricolour Square

111 **A** **B** **C**

Special abbreviations

beg cl = beginning cluster made from 5 dtr sts, **cl** = cluster made from 6 dtr sts

FOUNDATION RING: Using yarn A, work 8ch and join with ss to form a ring.

ROUND 1: 4ch *(counts as 1dtr)*, 5dtr, [3ch, 6dtr into ring] 3 times, 3ch, join with ss into 4th of 4ch.

ROUND 2: 4ch *(counts as 1dtr)*, beg cl into each of next 5dtr, * 5ch, ss into 2nd of 3ch, 5ch, ** cl into next 6dtr; rep from * twice and from * to ** once again, join with ss into 4th of 4ch. Break off yarn A.

ROUND 3: Join yarn B to top of any cl, * [3dtr, 1ch, 3dtr, 2ch, 3dtr, 1ch, 3dtr] into next 3ch sp of round 1, ss into top of next cl; rep from * 3 times, join with ss into top of first cl. Break off yarn B..

ROUND 4: Join yarn A to ss at top of any cl, 4ch *(counts as 1dtr)*, 5dtr into same place, * [6dtr, 2ch, 6dtr] into next 2ch sp, ** 6dtr into ss at top of next cl; rep from * twice, and from * to ** once again, join with ss into 4th of 4ch. Break off yarn A.

ROUND 5: Join yarn C to last ss of previous round, 1ch, 1dc into each of next 6dtr, 1tr into 1ch sp between groups of dtr worked on round 3, * 1dc into each of next 6dtr, 3dc into 2ch corner sp, ** [1dc into each of next 6dtr, 1tr into 1ch sp between groups of dtr worked on round 3] twice; rep from * twice and from * to ** once again, 1dc into each of next 6tr, 1tr into 1ch sp between groups of dtr worked on round 3, join with ss into first dc.

ROUND 6: 3ch *(counts as 1tr)*, 1tr into each dc and tr of previous round, working 3tr into centre st of each 3dc corner group, join with ss into 3rd of 3ch.

Fasten off yarn.

MIX-AND-MATCH

36 Pink Stripes

1
A **B** **C**
D

FOUNDATION CHAIN: Using yarn A, work 29ch.

FOUNDATION ROW: *(wrong side)* 1htr into 3rd ch from hook, 1htr into each ch, turn. *(27htr)*

ROW 1: 2ch *(counts as 1htr)*, 1htr into each htr, turn. *(27htr)*

ROWS 2 & 3: Rep row 1. Break off yarn A.

ROW 4: Join yarn B, 1ch, 1dc into each htr, turn. Break off yarn B.

ROW 5: Join yarn C, 2ch *(counts as 1htr)*, 1htr into each dc, turn.

ROWS 6 & 7: Rep row 1. Break off yarn C.

ROW 8: Join yarn D, rep row 4. Break off yarn D.

ROW 9: Join yarn A, rep row 5. Rep row 1 11 times.

Fasten off yarn.

MIX-AND-MATCH

37 Pin Stripes

1 ✂ Ⓐ Ⓑ

FOUNDATION RING: Using yarn A, work 4ch and join with ss to form a ring.

ROUND 1: 3ch *(counts as 1tr)*, 11tr into ring, join with ss into 3rd of 3ch. *(12 tr)*

ROUND 2: 3ch *(counts as 1tr)*, * [2tr, 1dtr] into next tr, [1dtr, 2tr] into next tr *(corner made)*, ** 1tr into next tr; rep from * twice and from * to ** once again, join with ss into 3rd of 3ch.

ROUND 3: 3ch *(counts as 1tr)*, 1tr into each of next 2tr, * [2tr, 1dtr] into next tr, [1dtr, 2tr] into next tr *(corner made)*, ** 1tr into each of next 5tr; rep from * twice and from * to ** once again, 1tr into each of next 2tr, join with ss into 3rd of 3ch. Break off yarn A.

ROUND 4: Join yarn B, 1ch, 1dc into same place, 1dc into each of next 4tr, * 2dc into each of next 2dtr, ** 1dc into each of next 9tr; rep from * twice and from * to ** once again, 1dc into each of next 4tr, join with ss into first dc. Break off yarn B.

ROUND 5: Join yarn A, 3ch *(counts as 1tr)*, 1tr into each of next 5dc, * [2tr, 1dtr] into next dc, [1dtr, 2tr] into next dc, ** 1tr into each of next 11dc; rep from * twice and from * to ** once again, 1tr into each of next 5dc, join with ss into 3rd of 3ch. Break off yarn A.

ROUND 6: Join yarn B, 1ch, 1dc into each tr of previous round, working 2dc into each dtr, join with ss into first dc. Break off yarn B.

ROUND 7: Join yarn A, 3ch *(counts as 1tr)*, 1tr into each of next 8dc, * [2tr, 1dtr] into next dc, [1dtr, 2tr] into next dc, ** 1tr into each of next 17dc; rep from * twice and from * to ** once again, 1tr into each of next 8dc, join with ss into 3rd of 3ch. Break off yarn A.

ROUND 8: Join yarn B and rep round 6. Break off yarn B.

ROUND 9: Join yarn A, 1ch, 1dc into each dc of previous round, working 2dc into each of two corner dc, join with ss into first dc.

Fasten off yarn.

MIX-AND-MATCH

 106 122 139

38 Dahlia

11 ✂ Ⓐ Ⓑ

Special abbreviations

beg pc = beginning popcorn made from 3ch and 3 tr sts, **pc** = popcorn made from 4 tr sts

FOUNDATION RING: Using yarn A, work 4ch and join with ss to form a ring.

ROUND 1: 4ch *(counts as 1tr, 1ch)*, [1tr into ring, 1ch] 11 times, join with ss into 3rd of 4ch.

ROUND 2: Ss into next 1ch sp, beg pc into same sp, 3ch, [pc into next 1ch sp, 3ch] 11 times, join with ss into top of beg pc.

ROUND 3: Ss into next 3ch sp, [beg pc, 3ch, pc] into same sp, [3ch, pc into next 3ch sp] twice, 3ch, * [pc, 3ch, pc] into next 3ch sp, [3ch, pc into next 3ch sp] twice, 3ch; rep from * twice , join with ss into top of beg pc.

ROUND 4: Ss into next 3ch sp, [beg pc, 4ch, pc] into same sp, [3ch, pc into next 3ch sp] 3 times, 3ch, * [pc, 4ch, pc] into next 3ch sp, [3ch, pc into next 3ch sp] 3 times, 3ch; rep from * twice , join with ss into top of beg pc. Break off yarn A.

ROUND 5: Join yarn B to any 4ch corner sp, 7ch *(counts as 1tr, 4ch)*, 1tr into same sp, [3ch, 1tr into next 3ch sp] 4 times, 3ch, * [1tr, 4ch, 1tr] into next 4ch sp, [3ch, 1tr into next 3ch sp] 4 times, 3ch; rep from * twice, join with ss into 3rd of 7ch.

ROUND 6: Ss into next 4ch sp, 3ch *(counts as 1tr)*, [1tr, 1dtr, 2tr] into same sp, * [1tr into next tr, 3tr into next 3ch sp] 5 times, 1tr into next tr, ** [2tr, 1dtr, 2tr] into next 4ch sp; rep from * twice and from * to ** once again, join with ss into 3rd of 3ch.

ROUND 7: 1ch, 1dc into each tr of previous round, working 3htr into dtr at each corner, join with ss into first dc.

Fasten off yarn.

MIX-AND-MATCH

 47 165 175

39 Gavin's Stripes

1 ☰
Ⓐ Ⓑ Ⓒ
Ⓓ Ⓔ

FOUNDATION CHAIN: Using yarn A, work 29ch.

FOUNDATION ROW: *(wrong side)* [1dc, 1ch, 1dc] into 2nd ch from hook, * miss 1ch [1dc, 1ch, 1dc] into next ch; rep from * to last ch, 1dc into last ch, turn.

ROW 1: 1ch, * [1dc, 1ch, 1dc] into first dc of each group of sts on previous row; rep from * to last st, 1dc into last st, turn.

Rep row 1, working the following colour sequence:

2 rows in A, 2 rows in B, 2 rows in C, 2 rows in D, 2 rows in E, 2 rows in A, 4 rows in B, 2 rows in E, 2 rows in C, 2 rows in A, 4 rows in E.

Fasten off yarn.

MIX-AND-MATCH

 154 169 179

40 Granny with a Twist

11 📷 Ⓐ Ⓑ Ⓒ

Special abbreviations

beg cl = beginning cluster made from 2 tr sts, **cl** = cluster made from 3 tr sts

FOUNDATION RING: Using yarn A, work 6ch and join with ss to form a ring.

ROUND 1: 3ch *(counts as 1tr)*, beg cl into ring, 3ch, [cl into ring, 3ch] 7 times, join with ss into top of beg cl. Break off yarn A.

ROUND 2: Join yarn B to any 3ch sp, 3ch *(counts as 1tr)*, [beg cl, 3ch, cl] into same sp, 1ch, * [cl, 3ch, cl] into next 3ch sp, 1ch; rep from * 6 times, join with ss into top of beg cl. Break off yarn B.

ROUND 3: Join yarn C to any 3ch sp, 3ch *(counts as 1tr)*, [2tr, 3ch, 3tr] into same sp, * 1ch, 3tr into next 3ch sp, 1ch, ** [3tr, 3ch, 3tr] into next 3ch sp; rep from * twice and from * to ** once again, join with ss into 3rd of 3ch.

ROUND 4: Ss in next 2tr and into next 3ch sp, 3ch *(counts as 1tr)*, [2tr, 3ch, 3tr] into same sp, * 1ch, [3tr into next 3ch sp, 1ch] twice, ** [3tr, 3ch, 3tr] into next 3ch sp; rep from * twice and from * to ** once again, join with ss into 3rd of 3ch.

ROUND 5: Ss in next 2tr and into next 3ch sp, 3ch *(counts as 1tr)*, [2tr, 3ch, 3tr] into same sp, * 1ch, [3tr into next 3ch sp, 1ch] 3 times, ** [3tr, 3ch, 3tr] into next 3ch sp; rep from * twice and from * to ** once again, join with ss into 3rd of 3ch.

ROUND 6: Ss in next 2tr and into next 3ch sp, 3ch *(counts as 1tr)*, [2tr, 3ch, 3tr] into same sp, * 1ch, [3tr into next 3ch sp, 1ch] 4 times, ** [3tr, 3ch, 3tr] into next 3ch sp; rep from * twice and from * to ** once again, join with ss into 3rd of 3ch.

ROUND 7: 1ch, 1dc into each tr and 1ch sp of previous round, working [2dc, 1ch, 2dc] into each 3ch corner sp, join with ss into first dc.

ROUND 8: 1ch, 1dc into each dc of previous round, working 3dc into each 1ch corner sp, join with ss into first dc.

Fasten off yarn.

MIX-AND-MATCH

 93 135 150

41 Bobble Triangle

11  A

Special abbreviation

MB = make bobble (work 4 open tr in same st leaving 5 loops on hook, draw yarn through all 5 loops at once)

FOUNDATION CHAIN: Work 28ch.

FOUNDATION ROW: *(wrong side)* Work 1dc into 2nd ch from hook, 1dc into each ch to end, turn. *(27dc)*

ROW 1: 1ch, 1dc into each dc, turn. *(27dc)*

ROW 2: 1ch, 1dc into each of next 24dc, MB, 1dc into each of next 2dc, turn.

ROW 3 and every alt row: Rep row 1.

ROW 4: 1ch, 1dc into each of next 21dc, MB, 1dc into each of next 5dc, turn.

ROW 6: 1ch, 1dc into each of next 18dc, MB, 1dc into each of next 5dc, MB, 1dc into each of next 2dc, turn.

ROW 8: 1ch, 1dc into each of next 15dc, MB, 1dc into each of next 5dc, MB, 1dc into each of next 5dc, turn.

ROW 10: 1ch, 1dc into each of next 12dc, [MB, 1dc into each of next 5dc] twice, MB, 1dc into each of next 2dc, turn.

ROW 12: 1ch, 1dc into each of next 9dc, [MB, 1dc into each of next 5dc] 3 times, turn.

ROW 14: 1ch, 1dc into each of next 6dc, [MB, 1dc into each of next 5dc] 3 times, MB, 1dc into each of next 2dc, turn.

ROW 16: 1ch, 1dc into each of next 3dc, [MB, 1dc into each of next 5dc] 4 times, turn.

ROW 18: Rep row 14.

ROW 20: Rep row 12.

ROW 22: Rep row 10.

ROW 24: Rep row 8.

ROW 26: Rep row 6.

ROW 28: Rep row 4.

ROW 30: Rep row 2.

ROWS 31 & 32: Rep row 1.

Fasten off yarn.

MIX-AND-MATCH

42 Lacy Wheel

1 A B C D

FOUNDATION RING: Using yarn A, work 8ch and join with ss to form a ring.

ROUND 1: 6ch *(counts as 1tr, 3ch)*, [1tr into ring, 3ch] 7 times, join with ss into 3rd of 6ch. *(8 spaced tr)*

ROUND 2: Ss into next 3ch sp, 3ch *(counts as 1tr)*, 3tr into same sp, [2ch, 4tr into next 3ch sp] 7 times, 2ch, join with ss into 3rd of 3ch. Break off yarn A.

ROUND 3: Join yarn B to any 2ch sp, 3ch *(counts as 1tr)*, 5tr into same sp, * 1ch, 6tr into next 2ch sp, 3ch, ** 6tr into next 2ch sp; rep from * twice and from * to ** once again, join with ss into 3rd of 3ch. Break off yarn B.

ROUND 4: Join yarn C to any 1ch sp, 1dc into same sp, * 3ch, 1dc between 3rd and 4th tr of next 6tr group, 3ch, [2tr, 3ch, 2tr] into next 3ch sp to make corner, 3ch, 1dc between 3rd and 4th tr of next 6tr group, 3ch, ** 1dc into next 1ch sp; rep from * twice and from * to ** once again, join with ss into first dc. Break off yarn C.

ROUND 5: Join yarn D to any 3ch corner sp, 3ch *(counts as 1tr)*, [1tr, 3ch, 2tr] into same sp, * [3ch, 1dc into next 3ch sp] 4 times, 3ch, ** [2tr, 3ch, 2tr] into next 3ch corner sp; rep from * twice and from * to ** once again, join with ss into 3rd of 3ch.

ROUND 6: Ss in next tr and into next 3ch corner sp, 3ch *(counts as 1tr)*, [2tr, 3ch, 3tr] into same sp, * [3ch, 1dc into next 3ch sp] 5 times, 3ch, ** [3tr, 3ch, 3tr] into next 3ch corner sp; rep from * twice and from * to ** once again, join with ss into 3rd of 3ch.

ROUND 7: Ss in next 2tr and into next 3ch corner sp, 3ch *(counts as 1tr)*, [2tr, 3ch, 3tr] into same sp, * [3ch, 1dc into next 3ch sp] 6 times, 3ch, ** [3tr, 3ch, 3tr] into next 3ch corner sp; rep from * twice and from * to ** once again, join with ss into 3rd of 3ch.

Fasten off yarn.

MIX-AND-MATCH

43 Four Patch Granny

11

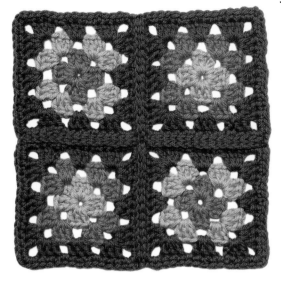

FOUNDATION RING: Using yarn A, work 6ch and join with ss to form a ring.

ROUND 1: 3ch *(counts as 1tr)*, 2tr into ring, 3ch, * 3tr into ring, 3ch; rep from * twice, join with ss into 3rd of 3ch. Break off yarn A.

ROUND 2: Join yarn B to any 3ch sp, 3ch *(counts as 1tr)*, [2tr, 3ch, 3tr] into same sp to make corner, * 1ch, [3tr, 3ch, 3tr] into next 3ch sp to make corner; rep from * twice, 1ch, join with ss into 3rd of 3ch. Break off yarn B.

ROUND 3: Join yarn C to any 3ch corner sp, 3ch *(counts as 1tr)*, [2tr, 3ch, 3tr] into same sp, * 1ch, 3tr into next 1ch sp, 1ch, [3tr, 3ch, 3tr] into next 3ch corner sp; rep from * to end, ending with 1ch, join with ss into 3rd of 3ch.

ROUND 4: 1ch, 1dc into every tr and 1ch sp of previous round, working [2dc, 1ch, 2dc] into each 3ch corner space, join with ss into first dc. Fasten off yarn.

Make 1 more patch using this colour combination.
Make 2 patches using yarn B instead of yarn A and yarn A instead of yarn B.
Using the photograph as a guide to position, join the patches together into a block of four using yarn B and the slip stitch method of joining shown on page 121.
Fasten off yarn.

MIX-AND-MATCH

44 Subtle Stripes

1

FOUNDATION CHAIN: Using yarn A, work 29ch.

FOUNDATION ROW: *(wrong side)* 1dc into 2nd ch from hook, 1dc into each ch, turn. *(28dc)*

ROW 1: 1ch, 1dc into each dc, turn. *(28dc)*

Rep row 1, working the following colour sequence:
1 more row in A, 3 rows in B, 3 rows in C, 3 rows in D, 3 rows in E, 4 rows in F, 3 rows in E, 3 rows in D, 3 rows in C, 3 rows in B, 3 rows in A.
Fasten off yarn.

MIX-AND-MATCH

45 Steps

11 ≣
A B

FOUNDATION CHAIN: Using yarn A, work 29ch.

WORKING THE PATTERN: When following the chart, read odd-numbered rows (right side rows) from right to left and even-numbered rows (wrong side rows) from left to right.

Starting at the bottom right-hand corner of the chart, work the 34 row pattern from the chart in dc. On the first row, work first dc into 2nd ch from hook, 1dc into each ch along row. *(28dc)*

Fasten off yarn.

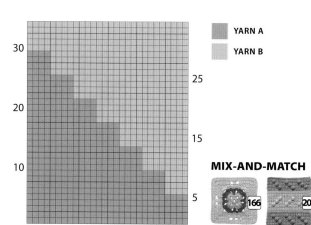

| | YARN A |
| | YARN B |

MIX-AND-MATCH

166   204   205

46 Meadow

11 A B C

Special abbreviations

beg pc = popcorn made from 3ch and 3 tr sts, **pc** = popcorn made from 4 tr sts

FOUNDATION RING: Using yarn A, work 4ch and join with ss to form a ring.

ROUND 1: Beg pc into ring, [3ch, pc into ring] 3 times, 3ch, join with ss into top of beg pc.

ROUND 2: 3ch *(counts as 1tr)*, [2tr, 3ch, 3tr] into next 3ch sp, 1ch, * [3tr, 3ch, 3tr] into next 3ch sp, 1ch; rep from * twice, join with ss into 3rd of 3ch.

ROUND 3: 1ch, 1dc into same place, 1dc into each of next 2tr, 5dc into next 3ch corner sp, * 1dc into each of next 3tr, 1dc into next ch, ** 1dc into each of next 3tr, 5dc into next 3ch corner sp; rep from * twice and from * to ** once again, join with ss into first dc. Break off yarn A.

ROUND 4: Join yarn B to first st of any 5dc corner group, 3ch *(counts as 1tr)*, * 1tr into next dc, [1tr, 2ch, 1tr] into next dc, 1tr into each of next 2dc, ** [1ch , miss 1dc, 1tr into next dc] 4 times; rep from * twice and from * to ** once again, [1ch, miss 1dc, 1tr into

next dc] 3 times, 1ch, join with ss into 3rd of 3ch. Break off yarn B.

ROUND 5: Join yarn C, 3ch *(counts as 1tr)*, * 1tr into each of next 2tr, [2tr, 2ch, 2tr] into next 2ch corner sp, 1tr into each of next 3tr, ** [1ch , 1tr into next tr] 4 times; rep from * twice and from * to ** once again, [1ch, 1tr into next tr] 3 times, 1ch, join with ss into 3rd of 3ch. Break off yarn C.

ROUND 6: Join yarn A, 3ch *(counts as 1tr)*, * 1tr into each of next 4tr, [2tr, 2ch, 2tr] into next 2ch corner sp, 1tr into each of next 5tr, ** [1ch , 1tr into next tr] 4 times; rep from * twice and from * to ** once again, [1ch, 1tr into next tr] 3 times, 1ch, join with ss into 3rd of 3ch. Break off yarn A.

ROUND 7: Join yarn C, 3ch *(counts as 1tr)*, * 1tr into each of next 6tr, [2tr, 2ch, 2tr] into next 2ch corner sp, 1tr into each of next 7tr, ** [1ch , 1tr into next tr] 4 times; rep from * twice and from * to ** once again, [1ch, 1tr into next tr] 3 times, 1ch, join with ss into 3rd of 3ch. Break off yarn C.

ROUND 8: Join yarn B, 3ch *(counts as 1tr)*, * 1tr into each of next 8tr, [2tr, 2ch, 2tr] into next 2ch corner sp, 1tr into each of next 9tr, ** [1ch , 1tr into next tr] 4 times; rep from * twice and from * to ** once again, [1ch, 1tr into next tr] 3 times, 1ch, join with ss into 3rd of 3ch.

Fasten off yarn.

MIX-AND-MATCH

 2   19   61

47 Queen Anne's Lace

11 📷 Ⓐ

Special abbreviations

beg cl = beginning cluster made from 3 tr sts, **cl** = cluster made from 4 tr sts

FOUNDATION RING: Using yarn A, work 6ch and join with ss to form a ring.

ROUND 1: 1ch, 12dc into ring, join with ss into first dc.

ROUND 2: 4ch *(counts as 1tr, 1ch)*, * 1tr into next dc, 1ch; rep from * 10 times, join with ss into 3rd of 4ch. *(12 spaced tr)*

ROUND 3: Ss into next 1ch sp, 3ch *(counts as 1tr)*, 2tr into same sp, 1ch, [3tr into next 1ch sp, 1ch] 11 times, join with ss into 3rd of 3ch.

ROUND 4: Ss in next 2tr and into next 1ch sp, 3ch *(counts as 1tr)*, beg cl into same sp, * 2ch, miss 1tr, 1tr into next tr, 2ch, ** cl into next 1ch sp; rep from * 10 times and from * to ** once again, join with ss into top of beg cl.

ROUND 5: Ss into next 2ch sp, 1ch, 3dc into same sp, [3dc into next 2ch sp] 23 times, join with ss into first dc.

ROUND 6: 3ch *(counts as 1tr)*, [1tr, 2ch, 2tr] into same place, * [2ch, miss next 3dc group, 1dc into sp between next two 3dc groups] 5 times, 2ch, ** [2tr, 2ch, 2tr] into sp above next cl; rep from * twice and from * to ** once again, join with ss into 3rd of 3ch.

ROUND 7: 3ch *(counts as 1tr)*, 1tr into next tr, * [2tr, 2ch, 2tr] into next 2ch corner sp, 1tr into each of next 2tr, [1tr, 1htr] into next 2ch sp, 1htr into next dc, [2dc into next 2ch sp, 1dc into next dc] 3 times, 2dc into next 2ch sp, 1htr into next dc, [1htr, 1tr] into next 2ch sp, ** 1tr into each of next 2tr; rep form * twice and from * to ** once again, join with ss into 3rd of 3ch.

ROUND 8: 3ch *(counts as 1tr)*, 1tr into each st of previous round, working [1tr, 1dtr, 1tr] into each 2ch corner sp, join with ss into 3rd of 3ch.

Fasten off yarn.

MIX-AND-MATCH

48 Danish Square

11 📷 Ⓐ Ⓑ Ⓒ Ⓓ

FOUNDATION RING: Using yarn A, work 10ch and join with ss to form a ring.

ROUND 1: 1ch, 20dc into ring, join with ss into first dc. *(20dc)*

ROUND 2: 9ch, * miss 4dc, 1dc into next dc, 8ch; rep from * twice, join with ss into first of 9ch.

ROUND 3: 1ch, 1dc into same place, [9dc into next 8ch sp, 1dc into next dc] 3 times, 9dc into next 8ch sp, join with ss into first dc. Break off yarn A.

ROUND 4: Join yarn B to 5th st of 9dc corner group, 1ch, 2dc into same place, [1dc into each of next 9dc, 2dc into next dc] 3 times, 1dc into each of next 9dc, join with ss into first dc. Break off yarn B.

ROUND 5: Join yarn C, 1ch, 2dc into same place, [1dc into each of next 10dc, 2dc into next dc] 3 times, 1dc into each of next 10dc, join with ss into first dc. Break off yarn C.

ROUND 6: Join yarn D, 4ch *(counts as 1tr, 1ch)*, 1tr into same place, * 1ch, [1tr into next dc, 1ch, miss 1dc] 5 times, 1tr into next dc, 1ch, ** [1tr, 1ch, 1tr] into next dc; rep from *

twice, and from * to ** once again, join with ss into 3rd of 4ch.

ROUND 7: Ss into next 1ch sp, 1ch, 3dc into same place, 1dc into next tr, * [1dc into 1ch sp, 1dc into next tr] 7 times, 3dc into next 1ch corner sp, 1dc into next tr; rep from * twice, [1dc into 1ch sp, 1dc into next tr] 6 times, join with ss into first dc. Break off yarn D.

ROUND 8: Join yarn A to centre st of any 3dc corner group, 1ch, 3dc into same place, 1dc into each dc of previous round, working 3dc into centre st of rem 3dc corner groups, join with ss into first dc. Break off yarn A.

ROUND 9: Join yarn C to centre st of any 3dc corner group, 4ch *(counts as 1tr, 1ch)*, 1tr into same place, * [1ch, miss 1dc, 1tr into next dc] 9 times, 1ch, ** miss 1dc, [1tr, 1ch, 1tr] into next dc; rep from * twice, and from * to ** once again, join with ss into 3rd of 4ch.

ROUND 10: 4ch *(counts as 1tr, 1ch)*, * [1tr, 1ch, 1tr, 1ch, 1tr] into next 1ch corner sp, ** [1ch, 1tr into next tr] 11 times, 1ch; rep from * twice and from * to ** once again, [1ch, 1tr into next tr] 10 times, 1ch, join with ss into 3rd of 4ch.

ROUND 11: 1ch, 1dc into same place, 1dc into each tr and 1ch sp of previous round, working 3dc into centre tr of each corner group, join with ss into first dc.

Fasten off yarn.

MIX-AND-MATCH

49 Rainbow Stripes

11

Ⓐ Ⓑ Ⓒ
Ⓓ Ⓔ Ⓕ
Ⓖ

Special abbreviations

dc3tog = decrease 2 sts by working the next 3 dc together

FOUNDATION CHAIN: Using yarn A, work 58ch.

FOUNDATION ROW: *(wrong side)* 1dc into 2nd ch from hook, 1dc into each ch, turn. *(57dc)*

ROW 1: 1ch, 1dc into each of next 27dc, dc3tog, 1dc into each of rem 27dc, turn. *(55dc)*

ROW 2: 1ch, 1dc into each of next 26dc, dc3tog, 1dc into each of rem 26dc, turn. *(53dc)*

ROW 3: 1ch, 1dc into each of next 25dc, dc3tog, 1dc into each of rem 25dc, turn. *(51dc)*

ROW 4: 1ch, 1dc into each of next 24dc, dc3tog, 1dc into each of rem 24dc, turn. *(49dc)* Break off yarn A. Join yarn B. Cont in pattern as set, working dc3tog over 3 centre sts on every row. At the same time, change yarn colours in the following colour sequence:

Work 4 rows in yarn B, 4 rows in yarn C, 4 rows in yarn D, 4 rows in yarn E, 4 rows in yarn F.

Join yarn G and cont in pattern until 3dc rem.

NEXT ROW: Work dc3tog.

Fasten off yarn.

MIX-AND-MATCH

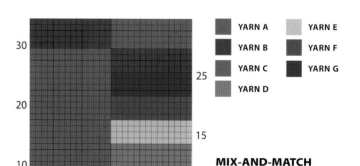

136 166 205

50 Seminole

11

Ⓐ Ⓑ Ⓒ
Ⓓ Ⓔ Ⓕ
Ⓖ

FOUNDATION CHAIN: Using yarn A, work 29ch.

WORKING THE PATTERN: When following the chart, read odd-numbered rows (right side rows) from right to left and even-numbered rows (wrong side rows) from left to right.

Starting at the bottom right-hand corner of the chart, work the 34 row pattern from the chart in dc. On the first row, work first dc into 2nd ch from hook, 1dc into each ch along row. *(28dc)*

Fasten off yarn.

	YARN A		YARN E
	YARN B		YARN F
	YARN C		YARN G
	YARN D		

30

25

20

15

10

5

MIX-AND-MATCH

172 181 201

51 Bright Flower

111 🔁

Ⓐ Ⓑ Ⓒ

52 Lemon Peel

1 ☰

Ⓐ

FOUNDATION RING: Using yarn A, work 6ch and join with ss to form a ring.

ROUND 1: 3ch (counts as 1tr), 3tr into ring, 3ch, turn; 1tr into first tr, 1tr into each of next 2tr, 1tr into 3rd of 3ch (petal made), 3ch, turn; * working across back of petal just made, 4tr into ring, 3ch, turn; 1tr into first tr, 1tr into each of next 3tr (petal made), 3ch, turn; rep from * 6 times, join with ss into 3rd of beg 3ch of first petal. Break off yarn A.

ROUND 2: Working behind the petals, join yarn B to any 3ch sp, 3ch (counts as 1tr), [2tr, 2ch, 3tr] into same sp, 3tr into next 3ch sp, * [3tr, 2ch, 3tr] into next 3ch sp, 3tr into next 3ch sp; rep from * twice, join with ss into 3rd of 3ch. Break off yarn B.

ROUND 3: Join yarn C to any 2ch corner sp, 3ch (counts as 1tr), [2tr, 3ch, 3tr] into same sp, * 1tr into each of next 9tr, ** [3tr, 3ch, 3tr] into next 2ch corner sp; rep from * twice and

from * to ** once again, join with ss into 3rd of 3ch.

ROUND 4: 3ch (counts as 1tr), 1tr into each of next 2tr, * [3tr, 3ch, 3tr] into 3ch corner sp, ** 1tr into each of next 15tr; rep from * twice and from * to ** once again, 1tr into each of next 12 tr, join with ss into 3rd of 3ch.

ROUND 5: 3ch (counts as 1tr), 1tr into each of next 5tr, * [3tr, 3ch, 3tr] into 3ch corner sp, ** 1tr into each of next 21tr; rep from * twice and from * to ** once again, 1tr into each of next 15 tr, join with ss into 3rd of 3ch.

ROUND 6: 1ch, 1dc into each tr of previous round, working 5dc into each 3ch corner sp, join with ss into first dc.

Fasten off yarn.

FOUNDATION CHAIN: Work 31ch.

FOUNDATION ROW: (right side) 1dc into 3rd ch from hook, * 1tr into next ch, 1dc into next ch; rep from * to end, turn.

ROW 1: 1ch, 1dc into first tr, 1tr into next dc, * 1dc into next tr, 1tr into next dc; rep from * to end, turn.

Rep row 1 21 times.

Fasten off yarn.

MIX-AND-MATCH

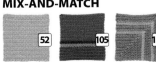

52   105   133

MIX-AND-MATCH

13   76   127

53 Mesh Fantasy

FOUNDATION CHAIN: Using yarn A, work 12ch.

FOUNDATION ROW: (wrong side) Work 1tr into 6th ch from hook (5 missed ch count as 1ch, 1tr, 1ch), [1ch, miss next ch, 1tr into next ch] 3 times, turn.

ROW 1: 4ch (counts as 1tr, 1ch), 1tr into next tr, [1ch, 1tr into next tr] twice, 1ch, miss next ch, 1tr into next ch, turn.

ROWS 2 & 3: Rep row 1. Break off yarn A.

Change from working rows to working in rounds.

ROUND 1: Holding square with row 3 at the top and right side facing, join yarn B to top right-hand corner sp and begin by working across row 4, 3ch (counts as 1tr), [2tr, 2ch, 3tr] into same sp (first corner made), 3tr into each of next 2 3ch sps, [3tr, 2ch, 3tr] into next sp (second corner made). Working into sps formed by edge tr and turning chs along next side of square, work 3tr into each of next 2 sps, [3tr, 2ch, 3tr] into next sp (third corner made). Working across foundation ch, work 3tr into each of

next 2 sps, [3tr, 2ch, 3tr] into next sp (fourth corner made). Working into sps formed by edge tr and turning chs along last side of square, work 3tr into each of next 2 sps, join with ss into 3rd of 3ch. Break off yarn B.

ROUND 2: Join yarn C to any 2ch corner sp, 3ch (counts as 1tr), [2tr, 2ch, 3tr] into same sp, * [2ch, miss next 3tr, 1tr between 3tr groups] 3 times, 2ch, ** [3tr, 2ch, 3tr] into next 2ch corner sp; rep from * twice and from * to ** once again, join with ss into 3rd of 3ch. Break off yarn C.

ROUND 3: Join yarn D to any 2ch corner sp, 3ch (counts as 1tr), [1tr, 2ch, 2tr] into same sp, * 1tr into each of next 3tr, [3tr into next 2ch sp] 4 times, 1tr into each of next 3tr, ** [2tr, 2ch, 2tr] into next 2ch corner sp; rep from * twice and from * to ** once again, join with ss into 3rd of 3ch. Break off yarn D.

ROUND 4: Join yarn B to any tr, 1ch, 1dc into each tr of previous round, working 3dc into each 2ch corner sp, join with ss into first dc. Break off yarn B.

ROUND 5: Join yarn A, 1ch, 1dc into each dc of previous round, working 3dc into centre st of each 3dc corner group, join with ss into first dc. Break off yarn A.

ROUND 6: Join yarn B and rep round 5.

Fasten off yarn.

MIX-AND-MATCH

54 Framed Flower

FOUNDATION CHAIN: Using yarn A, work 7ch.

ROUND 1: Work [1tr, 3ch] 3 times into 7th ch from hook (missed 6ch counts as 1tr, 3ch), join with ss into 3rd of 3ch.

ROUND 2: 1ch, 1dc into same place, * [1tr, 5dtr, 1tr] into next 3ch sp (petal made), ** 1dc into next tr; rep from * twice and from * to ** once again, join with ss into first dc.

ROUND 3: 1ch, 1dc into same place, * 1tr into next tr, 2tr into each of next 2dtr, 3tr into next dtr, 2tr into each of next 2dtr, 1tr into next tr, ** 1dc into next dc; rep from * twice and from * to ** once again, join with ss into first dc. Break off yarn A.

ROUND 4: Join yarn B to 4th tr of any petal, 1ch, 1dc into same place, * 5ch, miss next 5 sts, 1dc into next tr, 5ch, ** 1dc into 4th tr of next petal; rep from * twice and from * to ** once again, join with ss into first dc.

ROUND 5: Ss into next 5ch sp, 3ch (counts as 1tr), [3tr, 3ch, 4tr] into same 5ch sp, * 1ch, 7htr into next 5ch sp, 1ch, ** [4tr, 3ch, 4tr] into next 5ch sp; rep from * twice and from *

to ** once again, join with ss into 3rd of 3ch. Break off yarn B.

ROUND 6: Join yarn A to any 3ch corner sp, 2ch (counts as 1htr), [1htr, 2ch, 2htr] into same sp, * 1htr into each of next 4tr, miss 1ch sp, 1dc into each of next 7htr, miss 1ch sp, 1htr into each of next 4tr, ** [2htr, 2ch, 2htr] into next 3ch corner sp; rep from * twice and from * to ** once again, join with ss into 2nd of 2ch. Break off yarn A.

ROUND 7: Join yarn C to any 2ch corner sp, 3ch (counts as 1tr), [1tr, 2ch, 2tr] into same sp, * 1tr into each htr and dc along side of square, ** [2tr, 2ch, 2tr] into next 2ch corner sp; rep from * twice and from * to ** once again, join with ss into 3rd of 3ch.

ROUND 8: 3ch (counts as 1tr), 1tr into each tr of previous round, working 5tr into each 2ch corner sp, join with ss into 3rd of 3ch.

Fasten off yarn.

MIX-AND-MATCH

55 Centred Square

1 📷 Ⓐ Ⓑ Ⓒ

FOUNDATION RING: Using yarn A, work 4ch and join with ss to form a ring.

ROUND 1: 3ch (counts as 1tr), 2tr into ring, 2ch, [3tr into ring, 2ch] 3 times, join with ss into 3rd of 3ch.

ROUND 2: Ss in next 2tr and into next 2ch sp, 3ch (counts as 1tr), [2tr, 2ch, 3tr] into same sp, * [3tr, 2ch, 3tr] into next 2ch sp; rep from * twice, join with ss into 3rd of 3ch.

ROUND 3: Ss in next 2tr and into next 2ch sp, 3ch (counts as 1tr), [2tr, 2ch, 3tr] into same sp, * 3tr into sp between next two 3tr groups, ** [3tr, 2ch, 3tr] into next 2ch corner sp; rep from * twice and from * to ** once again, join with ss into 3rd of 3ch. Break off yarn A.

ROUND 4: Join yarn B to any 2ch corner sp, 3ch (counts as 1tr), [1tr, 2ch, 2tr] into same sp, * [1tr into each of next 3tr, 1tr into sp between next two 3tr groups] twice, 1tr into each of next 3tr, ** [2tr, 2ch, 2tr] into next 2ch corner sp; rep from * twice and from * to ** once again, join with ss into 3rd of 3ch. Break off yarn B.

ROUND 5: Join yarn A, 3ch (counts as 1tr), 1tr into next tr, * [2tr, 2ch, 2tr] into next 2ch corner sp, ** 1tr into each of next 15tr; rep from * twice and from * to ** once again, 1tr into each of next 13tr, join with ss into 3rd of 3ch. Break off yarn A.

ROUND 6: Join yarn C, 1ch, 1dc into same place, 1dc into each of next 3tr, * 3dc into next 2ch corner sp, ** 1dc into each of next 19tr; rep from * twice and from * to ** once again, 1dc into each of next 15tr, join with ss into first dc. Break off yarn C.

ROUND 7: Join yarn B, 3ch (counts as 1tr), 1tr into each of next 4dc, * [2tr, 2ch, 2tr] into centre st of 3dc corner group, ** 1tr into each of next 21dc; rep from * twice and from * to ** once again, 1tr into each of next 16dc, join with ss into 3rd of 3ch.

ROUND 8: 1ch, 1dc into each tr of previous round, working 5dc into each 2ch corner sp, join with ss into first dc.

Fasten off yarn.

MIX-AND-MATCH

56 Plain Granny

1 📷 Ⓐ

FOUNDATION RING: Work 4ch and join with ss to form a ring.

ROUND 1: 6ch (counts as 1tr, 3ch), [3tr into ring, 3ch] 3 times, 2tr into ring, join with ss into 3rd of 6ch.

ROUND 2: Ss into centre st of next 3ch sp, 6ch (counts as 1tr, 3ch), 3tr into same sp, * 1ch, [3tr, 3ch, 3tr] into next 3ch sp; rep from * twice, 1ch, 2tr into same sp as beg 6ch, join with ss into 3rd of 6ch.

ROUND 3: Ss into centre st of next 3ch sp, 6ch (counts as 1tr, 3ch), 3tr into same sp, * 1ch, 3tr into next 1ch sp, 1ch, ** [3tr, 3ch, 3tr] into next 3ch sp; rep from * twice and from * to ** once again, 2tr into same sp as beg 6ch, join with ss into 3rd of 6ch.

ROUND 4: Ss into centre st of next 3ch sp, 6ch (counts as 1tr, 3ch), 3tr into same sp, * 1ch, [3tr into next 1ch sp, 1ch] twice, ** [3tr, 3ch, 3tr] into next 3ch sp; rep from * twice and from * to ** once again, 2tr into same sp as beg 6ch, join with ss into 3rd of 6ch.

ROUND 5: Ss into centre st of next 3ch sp, 6ch (counts as 1tr, 3ch), 3tr into same sp, * 1ch, [3tr into next 1ch sp, 1ch] 3 times, ** [3tr, 3ch, 3tr] into next 3ch sp; rep from * twice and from * to ** once again, 2tr into same sp as beg 6ch, join with ss into 3rd of 6ch.

ROUND 6: Ss into centre st of next 3ch sp, 6ch (counts as 1tr, 3ch), 3tr into same sp, * 1ch, [3tr into next 1ch sp, 1ch] 4 times, ** [3tr, 3ch, 3tr] into next 3ch sp; rep from * twice and from * to ** once again, 2tr into same sp as beg 6ch, join with ss into 3rd of 6ch.

ROUND 7: Ss into centre st of next 3ch sp, 6ch (counts as 1tr, 3ch), 3tr into same sp, * 1ch, [3tr into next 1ch sp, 1ch] 5 times, ** [3tr, 3ch, 3tr] into next 3ch sp; rep from * twice and from * to ** once again, 2tr into same sp as beg 6ch, join with ss into 3rd of 6ch.

Fasten off yarn.

MIX-AND-MATCH

57 Arrowhead Bobbles

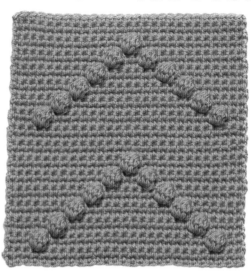

11

Special abbreviation

MB = make bobble (work 4 open tr in same st leaving 5 loops on hook, draw yarn through all 5 loops at once)

FOUNDATION CHAIN: Work 28ch.

FOUNDATION ROW: *(right side)* Work 1dc into 2nd ch from hook, 1dc into each ch to end, turn. *(27dc)*

ROW 1: 1ch, 1dc into each dc, turn. *(27dc)*

ROW 2: Rep row 1.

ROW 3: 1ch, 1dc into each of next 3dc, MB, 1dc into each of next 19dc, MB, 1dc into each of next 3dc, turn.

ROWS 4, 6, 8, 10, 12: Rep row 1.

ROW 5: 1ch, 1dc into each of next 5dc, MB, 1dc into each of next 15dc, MB, 1dc into each of next 5dc, turn.

ROW 7: 1ch, 1dc into each of next 7dc, MB, 1dc into each of next 11dc, MB, 1dc into each of next 7dc, turn.

ROW 9: 1ch, 1dc into each of next 9dc, MB, 1dc into each of next 7dc, MB, 1dc into each of next 9dc, turn.

ROW 11: 1ch, 1dc into each of next 11dc, MB, 1dc into each of next 3dc, MB, 1dc into each of next 11dc, turn.

ROW 13: 1ch, 1dc into each of next 13dc, MB, 1dc into each of next 13dc, turn.

ROWS 14 to 16: Rep row 1.

Rep rows 1 to 15 once again.

Fasten off yarn.

MIX-AND-MATCH

58 Peach Rose

11

FOUNDATION RING: Using yarn A, work 6ch and join with ss to form a ring.

ROUND 1: 1ch, 16 dc into ring, join with ss into first dc. *(16dc)*

ROUND 2: 6ch *(counts as 1tr, 3ch)*, miss 2dc, [1tr into next dc, 3ch, miss 1dc] 7 times, join with ss into 3rd of 6ch. *(8 spaced tr)*

ROUND 3: 1ch [1dc, 1htr, 3tr, 1htr, 1dc] into same sp, * [1dc, 1htr, 3tr, 1htr, 1dc] into next 3ch sp; rep from * 6 times, join with ss into first dc. *(8 petals made)* Break off yarn A.

ROUND 4: Join yarn B between any 2dc, 1ch, 1dc into same place, 6ch, [1dc between next 2dc, 6ch] 7 times, join with ss into first dc.

ROUND 5: 1ch [1dc, 1htr, 5tr, 1htr, 1dc] into same sp, * [1dc, 1htr, 5tr, 1htr, 1dc] into next 6ch sp; rep from * 6 times, join with ss into first dc. *(8 petals made)* Break off yarn B.

ROUND 6: Join yarn C to 2nd tr of any petal, 1ch, 1dc into same place, 6ch, miss 2tr, 1dc into next tr, [6ch, 1dc into 2nd tr of next petal, 6ch, miss 2tr, 1dc into next tr] 7 times, join with ss into first dc.

ROUND 7: Ss into next 6ch sp, 3ch *(counts as 1tr)*, [3tr, 4ch, 4tr] into same sp *(corner made)*, * 4ch, 1dc into next 6ch sp, [6ch, 1dc into next 6 ch sp] twice, 4ch, ** [4tr, 4ch, 4tr] into next 6ch sp *(corner made)*; rep from * twice and from * to ** once again, join with ss into 3rd of 3ch.

ROUND 8: 3ch *(counts as 1tr)*, 1tr into each of next 3 tr, * [3tr, 2ch, 3tr] into next 4ch corner sp, 1tr into each of next 4tr, 1ch, 2tr into next 4ch sp, [1ch, 3tr into next 6ch sp] twice, 1ch, 2tr into next 4ch sp, 1ch, ** 1tr into each of next 4tr; rep from * twice and from * to ** once again, join with ss into 3rd of 3ch.

Fasten off yarn.

MIX-AND-MATCH

59 Coral Quartet

11 ≣
Ⓐ Ⓑ Ⓒ
Ⓓ

FOUNDATION CHAIN: Using yarn A, work 29ch.

WORKING THE PATTERN: When following the chart, read odd-numbered rows (right side rows) from right to left and even-numbered rows (wrong side rows) from left to right.

Starting at the bottom right-hand corner of the chart, work the 34 row pattern from the chart in dc. On the first row, work first dc into 2nd ch from hook, 1dc into each ch along row. *(28dc)*

Fasten off yarn.

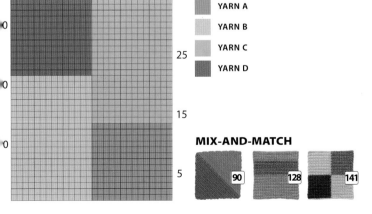

	YARN A
	YARN B
	YARN C
	YARN D

25

15

5

MIX-AND-MATCH

90   128   141

60 Popcorn Corners

11 📷 Ⓐ Ⓑ Ⓒ Ⓓ

Special abbreviation

pc = popcorn made from 5 tr sts

FOUNDATION RING: Using yarn A, work 4ch and join with ss to form a ring.

ROUND 1: 3ch *(counts as 1tr)*, 3tr into ring, 1ch, [4tr into ring, 1ch] 3 times, join with ss into 3rd of 3ch. Break off yarn A.

ROUND 2: Join yarn B to any 1ch sp, 3ch *(counts as 1tr)*, [3tr, 1ch, 4tr] into same sp, 1ch, * [4tr, 1ch, 4tr] into next 1ch sp, 1ch; rep from * twice, join with ss into 3rd of 3ch. Break off yarn B.

ROUND 3: Join yarn C to any 1ch corner sp, 3ch *(counts as 1tr)*, [1tr, pc, 2tr] into same sp, * miss 1tr, 1tr into each of next 3tr, 1tr into 1ch sp, 1tr into each of next 3tr, miss 1tr, ** [2tr, pc, 2tr] into next 1ch corner sp; rep from * twice and from * to ** once again, join with ss into 3rd of 3ch. Break off yarn C.

ROUND 4: Join yarn B to centre tr on any side of square, 3ch *(counts as 1tr)*, 1tr into each of next 6tr, * [1tr, 2dtr, 1tr] into top of next pc, ** 1tr into each of next 11tr; rep from * twice and from * to ** once again, 1tr into each of next 4tr, join with ss into 3rd of 3ch. Break off yarn B.

ROUND 5: Join yarn D, 3ch *(counts as 1tr)*, 1tr into each of next 7tr, * [2tr, 1dtr] into first dtr, [1dtr, 2tr] into next dtr, ** 1tr into each of next 13tr; rep from * twice and from * to ** once again, 1tr into each of next 5tr, join with ss into 3rd of 3ch. Break off yarn D.

ROUND 6: Join yarn C, 3ch *(counts as 1tr)*, 1tr into each of next 9tr, * 2tr into first dtr, pc between this dtr and next dtr, 2tr into next dtr, ** 1tr into each of next 17tr; rep from * twice and from * to ** once again, 1tr into each of next 7tr, join with ss into 3rd of 3ch. Break off yarn C.

ROUND 7: Join yarn B, 1ch, 1dc into same place, 1dc into each of next 12tr, * 2ch, miss next pc, ** 1dc into each of next 21tr; rep from * twice and from * to ** once again, 1dc into each of next 8tr, join with ss into first dc.

ROUND 8: 1ch, 1dc into each dc of previous round, working [2htr, 1tr, 2htr] into each 2ch corner sp, join with ss into first dc.

Fasten off yarn.

MIX-AND-MATCH

 114 132 192

61 Nine Patch Granny

11 📷
Ⓐ Ⓑ Ⓒ
Ⓓ Ⓔ

62 Edged Square

11 ≋
Ⓐ Ⓑ

FOUNDATION RING: Using yarn A, work 6ch and join with ss to form a ring.

ROUND 1: 3ch (counts as 1tr), 2tr into ring, 3ch, * 3tr into ring, 3ch; rep from * twice more, join with ss into 3rd of 3ch. Break off yarn A.

ROUND 2: Join yarn B to any 3ch sp, 3ch (counts as 1tr), [2tr, 3ch, 3tr] into same sp to make corner, * 1ch, [3tr, 3ch, 3tr] into next 3ch sp to make corner; rep from * twice more, 1ch, join with ss into 3rd of 3ch.

Fasten off yarn.

Make 3 more patches using this colour combination.

Make 2 patches using yarn C instead of yarn A.

Make 2 patches using yarn D instead of yarn A.

Make 1 patch using yarn E instead of yarn A.

Using the photograph as a guide to position, join the patches together into a block of nine using yarn B

and the slip stitch method of joining shown on page 121.

EDGING ROUND: Join yarn B to any tr along one edge of the block, 1ch, 1dc into each tr and ch round edge, working 3dc into centre ch at each corner, join with ss into first dc.

Fasten off yarn.

Special abbreviation

dc3tog = decrease 2 sts by working the next 3 dc together

FOUNDATION CHAIN: Using yarn A, work 58ch.

FOUNDATION ROW: (wrong side) 1dc into 2nd ch from hook, 1dc into each ch, turn. (57dc)

ROW 1: 1ch, 1dc into each of next 27dc, dc3tog, 1dc into each of rem 27dc, turn. (55dc)

ROW 2: 1ch, 1dc into each of next 26dc, dc3tog, 1dc into each of rem 26dc, turn. (53dc)

ROW 3: 1ch, 1dc into each of next 25dc, dc3tog, 1dc into each of rem 25dc, turn. (51dc)

ROW 4: 1ch, 1dc into each of next 24dc, dc3tog, 1dc into each of rem 24dc, turn. (49dc)

Cont in pattern as set, working dc3tog over 3 centre sts on every row.

Work 2 more rows in yarn A. Break off yarn A.

Join yarn B and cont in pattern until 3dc rem.

NEXT ROW: Work dc3tog.

Fasten off yarn.

MIX-AND-MATCH

 2
 45
 127

MIX-AND-MATCH

 1
76
96

63 Random Patches

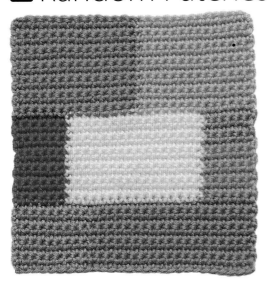

11 ☰
Ⓐ Ⓑ Ⓒ
Ⓓ Ⓔ Ⓕ

64 Sunshine Lace

1 🔄
Ⓐ

FOUNDATION CHAIN: Using yarn A, work 29ch.

WORKING THE PATTERN: When following the chart, read odd-numbered rows (right side rows) from right to left and even-numbered rows (wrong side rows) from left to right.
Starting at the bottom right-hand corner of the chart, work the 34 row pattern from the chart in dc. On the first row, work first dc into 2nd ch from hook, 1dc into each ch along row. *(28dc)*
Fasten off yarn.

FOUNDATION RING: Work 8ch and join with ss to form a ring.

ROUND 1: 1ch, 12dc into ring, join with ss into first dc. *(12dc)*

ROUND 2: 6ch *(counts as 1dtr, 2ch)*, [1dtr into next st, 2ch] 11 times, join with ss into 4th of 6ch.
(12 spaced dtr)

ROUND 3: 5ch *(counts as 1tr, 2ch)*, * [1dc into next 2ch sp, 2ch] twice, [3tr, 2ch, 3tr] into next 2ch sp, 2ch; rep from * 3 times omitting 1tr, 2ch at end of last rep, join with ss into 3rd of 5ch.

ROUND 4: 1ch, * [1dc into next 2ch sp, 2ch] 3 times, [3tr, 2ch, 3tr] into 2ch corner sp, 2ch; rep from * 3 times, join with ss into first dc.

ROUND 5: Ss into next 2ch sp, 1ch, 1dc into same sp, 2ch, [1dc into next 2ch sp, 2ch] twice, * [3tr, 2ch, 3tr] into next 2ch corner sp, 2ch, ** [1dc into next 2ch sp, 2ch] 4 times; rep from * twice and from * to ** once again, 1dc into next 2ch sp, 2ch, join with ss into first dc.

ROUND 6: Ss into next 2ch sp, 3ch *(counts as 1tr)*, 1tr into same sp, work 2tr into each 2ch sp on previous round, working 1tr into each tr and [3tr, 2ch, 3tr] into each 2ch corner sp, join with ss into 3rd of 3ch.

ROUND 7: 3ch *(counts as 1tr)*, work 1tr into each tr on previous round, working 5tr into each 2ch corner sp, join with ss into 3rd of 3ch.
Fasten off yarn.

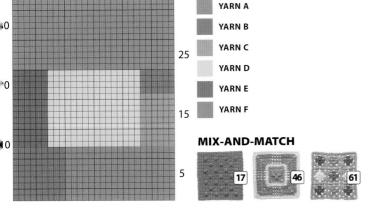

	YARN A
	YARN B
	YARN C
	YARN D
	YARN E
	YARN F

MIX-AND-MATCH

17 46 61

MIX-AND-MATCH

 3 74 131

65 Patriotic Sunburst

66 Abstract

11 📷 A B C

Special abbreviations

beg cl = beginning cluster made from 1 tr st, **cl** = cluster made from 2 tr sts

---

FOUNDATION RING: Using yarn A, work 4ch and join with ss to form a ring.

ROUND 1: 1ch, 6dc into ring, join with ss into first dc.

ROUND 2: 1ch, 2dc into next dc 6 times, join with ss into first dc. (12dc)

ROUND 3: 1ch, 2dc into next dc 12 times, join with ss into first dc. (24dc) Break off yarn A.

ROUND 4: Join yarn B to any dc, 3ch (counts as 1tr), beg cl into same dc, 2ch, miss next dc, * cl into next dc, 2ch, miss next dc; rep from * 10 times, join with ss into top of beg cl. Break off yarn B.

ROUND 5: Join yarn C to any 2ch sp, 3ch (counts as 1tr), beg cl into same sp, 3ch, * cl into next 2ch sp, 3ch; rep from * 10 times, join with ss into top of beg cl.

ROUND 6: 1ch, 1dc into top of beg cl, 3dc into next 3ch sp, * 1dc into top of next cl, 3dc into next 3ch sp; rep from * 10 times, join with ss into first dc. Break off yarn C.

ROUND 7: Join yarn A to centre st of any 3dc group, 3ch (counts as 1tr), 2tr into same dc (corner made), * 1htr into each of next 2dc, 1dc into each of next 7dc, 1htr into each of next 2dc, ** 3tr into next dc (corner made); rep from * twice and from * to ** once again, join with ss into 3rd of 3ch. Break off yarn A.

ROUND 8: Join yarn B to centre st of any 3tr corner group, 4ch (counts as 1dtr), 2dtr into same tr, * 1tr into each of next 2 sts, 1htr into each of next 9 sts, 1tr into each of next 2 sts, ** 3dtr into next st; rep from * twice and from * to ** once again, join with ss into 4th of 4ch.

ROUND 9: 1ch, 1dc into same place, * 3dc into next dtr, 1dc into each of next 15 sts; rep from * 3 times, ending last rep with 1dc into each of next 14 sts, join with ss into first dc. Break off yarn B.

ROUND 10: Join yarn C to any dc along one side of square, 1ch, work 1dc into each dc of previous round, working 3dc into centre st of each 3dc corner group, join with ss into first dc. Break off yarn C.

ROUND 11: Join yarn A, 3ch (counts as 1tr), work 1tr into each dc of previous round, working [2tr, 2ch, 2tr] into centre st of each 3dc corner group, join with ss into 3rd of 3ch. Break off yarn A.

ROUND 12: Join yarn B, 1ch, work 1dc into each tr of previous round, working 3dc into each 2ch corner sp, join with ss into first dc.
Fasten off yarn.

MIX-AND-MATCH

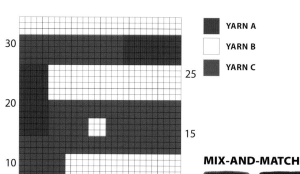

11 ≣
A B C

FOUNDATION CHAIN: Using yarn A, work 29ch.

WORKING THE PATTERN: When following the chart, read odd-numbered rows (right side rows) from right to left and even-numbered rows (wrong side rows) from left to right.

Starting at the bottom right-hand corner of the chart, work the 34 row pattern from the chart in dc. On the first row, work first dc into 2nd ch from hook, 1dc into each ch along row. (28dc)

Fasten off yarn.

■ YARN A
□ YARN B
■ YARN C

MIX-AND-MATCH

67 American Beauty

111 [icons] **A** B **C**

FOUNDATION RING: Using yarn A, work 12ch and join with ss to form a ring.

ROUND 1: 1ch, 18dc into ring, join with ss into first dc.

ROUND 2: 1ch, 1dc into same place, [3ch, miss 2dc, 1dc into next dc] 5 times, 3ch, miss 2dc, join with ss into first dc. *(6 3ch loops)*

ROUND 3: 1ch, [1dc, 3ch, 5tr, 3ch, 1dc] into each of next 6 3ch loops, join with ss into first dc. *(6 petals)*

ROUND 4: 1ch, 1dc into same place, [5ch behind petal of previous round, 1dc between 2dc] 5 times, 5ch behind petal of previous round, join with ss into first dc. *(6 5ch loops)*

ROUND 5: 1ch, [1dc, 3ch, 7tr, 3ch, 1dc] into each of next 6 5ch loops, join with ss into first dc. *(6 petals)*

ROUND 6: 1ch, 1dc into same place, [7ch behind petal of previous round, 1dc between 2dc] 5 times, 7ch behind petal of previous round, join with ss into first dc. *(6 7ch loops)*

ROUND 7: 1ch, [1dc, 3ch, 9tr, 3ch, 1dc] into each of next 6 7ch loops, join with ss into first dc. *(6 petals)* Break off yarn A.

ROUND 8: Join yarn B between any 2dc, 1ch, [1dc between 2dc, 8ch behind petal of previous round] 6 times, join with ss into first dc. *(6 8ch loops)*

ROUND 9: Ss into next 8ch loop, 3ch *(counts as 1tr)*, [7tr, 2ch, 3tr] into same loop, * 10tr into next 8ch loop, [3tr, 2ch, 8tr] into next 8ch loop, ** [8tr, 2ch, 3tr] into next 8ch loop; rep from * to ** once, join with ss into 3rd of 3ch. *(16tr along each side of square)*

ROUND 10: 3ch *(counts as 1tr)*, 1tr into each tr of previous round, working [3tr, 2ch, 3tr] into each 2ch corner sp, join with ss into 3rd of 3ch. Break off yarn B.

ROUND 11: Join yarn C, 3ch *(counts as 1tr)*, 1tr into each tr of previous round, working [2tr, 2ch, 2tr] into each 2ch corner sp, join with ss into 3rd of 3ch.

ROUND 12: 1ch, 1dc into each tr of previous round, working 3dc into each 2ch corner sp, join with ss into first dc.

Fasten off yarn.

MIX-AND-MATCH

 65 66 68

68 Red, White & Blue

1 [icon] **A** B **C**

FOUNDATION CHAIN: Using yarn A, work 6ch.

ROW 1: *(right side)* Insert hook into 4th ch from hook, work 3tr, turn.

ROW 2: 3ch *(counts as 1tr)*, 1tr into each of next 2tr, 4tr into loop made by turning ch of previous row, turn.

ROW 3: 3ch *(counts as 1tr)*, 1tr into each of next 2tr, [2tr, 2ch, 2tr] into next tr, 1tr into each of next 2tr, 1tr into 3rd of 3 ch, turn.

ROW 4: 3ch *(counts as 1tr)*, 1 tr into each of next 4tr, [2tr, 2ch, 2tr] into 2ch sp, 1tr into each of next 4tr, 1tr into 3rd of 3ch, turn.

ROW 5: 3ch *(counts as 1tr)*, 1 tr into each of next 6tr, [2tr, 2ch, 2tr] into 2ch sp, 1tr into each of next 6tr, 1tr into 3rd of 3ch, turn. Break off yarn A.

ROW 6: Join yarn B, 3ch *(counts as 1tr)*, 1 tr into each of next 8tr, [2tr, 2ch, 2tr] into 2ch sp, 1tr into each of next 8tr, 1tr into 3rd of 3ch, turn.

ROW 7: 3ch *(counts as 1tr)*, 1 tr into each of next 10tr, [2tr, 2ch, 2tr] into 2ch sp, 1tr into each of next 10tr, 1tr into 3rd of 3ch, turn.

ROW 8: 3ch *(counts as 1tr)*, 1 tr into each of next 12tr, [2tr, 2ch, 2tr] into 2ch sp, 1tr into each of next 12tr, 1tr into 3rd of 3ch, turn.

ROW 9: Join yarn A, 3ch *(counts as 1tr)*, 1 tr into each of next 14tr, [2tr, 2ch, 2tr] into 2ch sp, 1tr into each of next 14tr, 1tr into 3rd of 3ch, turn. Break off yarn B.

ROW 10: Join yarn C, 3ch *(counts as 1tr)*, 1 tr into each of next 16tr, [2tr, 2ch, 2tr] into 2ch sp, 1tr into each of next 16tr, 1tr into 3rd of 3ch, turn.

ROW 11: 3ch *(counts as 1tr)*, 1 tr into each of next 18tr, [2tr, 2ch, 2tr] into 2ch sp, 1tr into each of next 18tr, 1tr into 3rd of 3ch.

ROW 12: 3ch *(counts as 1tr)*, 1 tr into each of next 20tr, [2tr, 2ch, 2tr] into 2ch sp, 1tr into each of next 20tr, 1tr into 3rd of 3ch, turn.

ROW 13: 3ch *(counts as 1tr)*, 1 tr into each of next 22tr, [2tr, 2ch, 2tr] into 2ch sp, 1tr into each of next 22tr, 1tr into 3rd of 3ch, turn.

ROW 14: 3ch *(counts as 1tr)*, 1 tr into each of next 24tr, 5tr into 2ch sp, 1tr into each of next 24tr, 1tr into 3rd of 3ch.

Fasten off yarn.

MIX-AND-MATCH

 65 66 67

69 Fudge

11 A B C D E

Special abbreviations

beg cl = beginning cluster made from 3 tr sts, **cl** = cluster made from 4 tr sts

---

FOUNDATION RING: Using yarn A, work 6ch and join with ss to form a ring.

ROUND 1: 1ch, 12dc into ring, join with ss into first dc. Break off yarn A.

ROUND 2: Join yarn B to any dc, 4ch *(counts as 1tr, 1ch)*,* 1tr into next dc, 1ch; rep from * 10 times, join with ss into 3rd of 4ch. *(12 spaced tr)* Break off yarn B.

ROUND 3: Join yarn C to any 1ch sp, 3ch *(counts as 1tr)*, beg cl into same sp, 3ch,* cl into next 1ch sp, 3ch; rep from * 10 times, join with ss into top of beg cl. *(12 clusters)* Break off yarn C.

ROUND 4: Join yarn D to any 3ch sp, 3ch *(counts as 1tr)*, beg cl into same sp,* 2ch, 1tr into top of next cl, 2ch,** cl into next 3ch sp; rep from * 10 times and from * to ** once again, join with ss into top of beg cl. Break off yarn D.

ROUND 5: Join yarn A to any 2ch sp, 1ch, 3dc into each 2ch sp of previous round, join with ss into first dc. Break off yarn A.

ROUND 6: Join yarn C to top of any cl, 3ch *(counts as 1tr)*, [1tr, 2ch, 2tr] into same place,* [2ch, miss next 3dc group, 1dc into sp between next two 3dc groups] 5 times, 2ch,** [2tr, 2ch, 2tr] into sp above next cl; rep from * twice and from * to ** once again, join with ss into 3rd of 3ch. Break off yarn C.

ROUND 7: Join yarn E into first tr of any corner group, 3ch *(counts as 1tr)*, 1tr into next tr,* [2tr, 2ch, 2tr] into 2ch corner sp, 1tr into each of next 2tr, 2ch, 1tr into next dc, [2ch, 1dc into next dc] 3 times, 2ch, 1tr into next dc, 2ch,** 1tr into each of next 2tr; rep from * twice and from * to ** once again, join with ss into 3rd of 3ch. Break off yarn E.

ROUND 8: Join yarn D to any 2ch corner sp, 1ch, 3dc into same sp,* 1dc into each of next 4tr, 2ch, 1dc into next tr, [2ch, 1dc into next dc] 3 times, 2ch, 1dc into next tr, 2ch, 1dc into each of next 4tr,** 3dc into next 2ch corner sp; rep from * twice and from * to ** once again, join with ss into first dc. Break off yarn D.

ROUND 9: Join yarn B to centre st of any 3dc corner group, 1ch, 3dc into same place,* 1dc into each of next 5dc, [2ch, 1dc into next dc] 5 times, 2ch, 1dc into each of next 5dc,** 3dc into centre st of next 3dc corner group; rep from * twice and from * to ** once again, join with ss into first dc. Break off yarn B.

ROUND 10: Join yarn C to any dc along side of square, 1ch, 1dc into each dc of previous round, working 3dc into centre st of each 3dc corner group and 2dc into each 2ch sp, join with ss into first dc. Fasten off yarn.

MIX-AND-MATCH

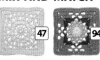

47   94   145

70 ZigZag

11 A B C

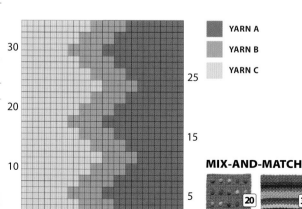

FOUNDATION CHAIN: Using yarn A, work 29ch.

WORKING THE PATTERN: When following the chart, read odd-numbered rows (right side rows) from right to left and even-numbered rows (wrong side rows) from left to right.

Starting at the bottom right-hand corner of the chart, work the 34 row pattern from the chart in dc. On the first row, work first dc into 2nd ch from hook, 1dc into each ch along row. *(28dc)*

Fasten off yarn.

YARN A
YARN B
YARN C

MIX-AND-MATCH

20   39   169

71 StarFlower

11
A B

72 Ribbed Square

1
A

FOUNDATION RING: Using yarn A, work 4ch and join with ss to form a ring.

ROUND 1: 1ch, 8dc into ring, join with ss into first dc.

ROUND 2: * 6ch, 1dc into 3rd ch from hook and in next ch, 1htr into each of next 2ch, ss into next dc *(petal made)*; rep from * 7 times, join with ss into first of 6ch. *(8 petals)* Break off yarn A.

ROUND 3: Join yarn B to tip of any petal, 5ch *(counts as 1tr, 2ch)*, 1tr into same place *(corner made)*, 4ch, ss into tip of next petal, 4ch, * [1tr, 2ch, 1tr] into tip of next dc *(corner made)*, 4ch, ss into tip of next petal, 4ch; rep from * twice, join with ss into 3rd of 5ch.

ROUND 4: Ss into next 2ch corner sp, 3ch *(counts as 1tr)*, [2tr, 2ch, 3tr] into same 2ch sp, 4tr into each of next 2 4ch sps, * [3tr, 2ch, 3tr] into next 2ch corner sp, 4tr into each of next 2 4ch sps; rep from * twice, join with ss into 3rd of 3ch.

ROUND 5: 3ch *(counts as 1tr)*, 1tr into each tr of previous round, working [3tr, 2ch, 3tr] into each 2ch corner sp, join with ss into 3rd of 3ch. Break off yarn B.

ROUND 6: Join yarn A, 3ch *(counts as 1tr)*, 1tr into each tr of previous round, working [3tr, 2ch, 3tr] into each 2ch corner sp, join with ss into 3rd of 3ch. Break off yarn A.

ROUND 7: Join yarn B, 3ch *(counts as 1tr)*, 1tr into each tr of previous round, working 5tr into each 2ch corner sp, join with ss into 3rd of 3ch.

Fasten off yarn.

FOUNDATION CHAIN: Using yarn A, work 29ch.

FOUNDATION ROW: *(wrong side)* 1dc into 2nd ch from hook, 1dc into each ch, turn. *(28dc)*

ROW 1: 1ch, working only into the back loop of each stitch, 1dc into each dc, turn. *(28dc)*

Rep row 1 32 times.

Fasten off yarn.

MIX-AND-MATCH

 2
 38
165

MIX-AND-MATCH

 102
 154
 175

73 Catherine Wheel

11 📷 Ⓐ Ⓑ Ⓒ

FOUNDATION RING: Using yarn A, work 6ch and join with ss to form a ring.

ROUND 1: 3ch (counts as 1tr), 19tr into ring, join with ss into 3rd of 3ch. (20tr) Break off yarn A.

ROUND 2: Join yarn B to any tr, 4ch (counts as 1tr, 1ch), [1tr into next tr, 1ch] 19 times, join with ss into 3rd of 3ch. (20 spaced tr) Break off yarn B.

ROUND 3: Join yarn C to any 1ch sp, 3ch (counts as 1tr), 2tr into same sp, [3tr into next 1ch sp] 3 times, 5ch, * miss next 1ch sp, [3tr into next 1ch sp] 4 times, 5ch; rep from * twice, join with ss into 3rd of 3ch. Break off yarn C.

ROUND 4: Join yarn A to any tr, 1tr into each tr of previous round, working [3tr, 2ch, 3tr] into each 5ch corner sp, join with ss into 3rd of 3ch. Break off yarn A.

ROUND 5: Join yarn B to any 2ch corner sp, 3ch (counts as 1tr), [2tr, 2ch, 3tr] into same sp, * [2ch, miss 2tr, 1tr into next tr] 3 times, [1tr into next tr, 2ch, miss 2tr] 3 times, ** [3tr, 2ch, 3tr] into next 2ch corner sp; rep from * twice and from * to ** once again, join with ss into 3rd of 3ch.

ROUND 6: 3ch (counts as 1tr), 1tr into each of next 2tr, * [3tr, 2ch, 3tr] into same sp, 1tr into each of next 3tr, [2ch, 1tr into next tr] 3 times, [1tr into next tr, 2ch] 3 times, ** 1tr into each of next 3tr; rep from * twice and from * to ** once again, join with ss into 3rd of 3ch.

ROUND 7: 1ch, 1dc into each tr of previous round, working 2dc into each 2ch sp along sides of square and 3dc into each 2ch corner sp; join with ss into first dc.

Fasten off yarn.

MIX-AND-MATCH

 96 151 209

74 Seville

11 📷 Ⓐ

FOUNDATION RING: Using yarn A, work 8ch and join with ss to form a ring.

ROUND 1: 3ch (counts as 1tr), 2tr into ring, 7ch, [3tr into ring, 7ch] 7 times, join with ss into 3rd of 3ch.

ROUND 2: Ss into next 7ch sp, 3ch (counts as 1tr), [2tr, 2ch, 3tr] into same sp, * 7ch, miss next 7ch sp, [3tr, 2ch, 3tr] into next 7ch sp; rep from * twice, 7ch, miss next 7ch sp, join with ss into 3rd of 3ch.

ROUND 3: 3ch (counts as 1tr), 1tr into each of next 2tr, * [2tr, 2ch, 2tr] into 2ch corner sp, 1tr into each of next 3tr, 7ch, ** 1tr into each of next 3tr; rep from * twice and from * to ** once again, join with ss into 3rd of 3ch.

ROUND 4: 3ch (counts as 1tr), 1tr into each of next 4tr, * [2tr, 2ch, 2tr] into 2ch corner sp, 1tr into each of next 5tr, 4ch, 1dc into missed 7ch sp of round 1 enclosing ch made on rounds 2 and 3, 4ch, ** 1tr into each of next 5tr; rep from * twice and from * to ** once again, join with ss into 3rd of 3ch.

ROUND 5: 1ch, 1dc into same place, 1dc into each of next 6tr, *3 dc into next 2ch corner sp, 1dc into each of next 7tr, 1dc into next 4ch sp, 3ch, 1dc into next 4ch sp, ** 1dc into each of next 7tr; rep from * twice and from * to ** once again, join with ss into first dc.

ROUND 6: 4ch (counts as 1tr, 1ch), * [miss 1dc, 1tr into next dc, 1ch] 3 times, 5tr into centre st of next 3dc corner group, 1ch, [miss 1dc, 1tr into next dc, 1ch] 3 times, miss next dc, 1tr into each of next 2dc, 2tr into next 3ch sp, ** 1tr into each of next 2dc; rep from * twice and from * to ** once again, 1tr into next dc, join with ss into 3rd of 4ch.

ROUND 7: 4ch (counts as 1tr, 1ch), * [1tr into next dc, 1ch] 3 times, 1tr into each of next 2tr, 3tr into centre st of 5tr corner group, 1tr into each of next 2tr, 1ch, [1tr into next dc, 1ch] 3 times, ** 1tr into each of next 6tr; rep from * twice and from * to ** once again, 1tr into each of next 5tr, join with ss into 3rd of 4ch.

Fasten off yarn.

MIX-AND-MATCH

 166 190 200

75 Half & Half

1 ☰
Ⓐ Ⓑ

FOUNDATION CHAIN: Using yarn A, work 32ch.

FOUNDATION ROW: *(wrong side)* 1tr into 4th ch from hook, 1tr into each ch to end, turn. *(30tr)*

ROW 1: 3ch *(counts as 1tr)*, 1tr into each tr of previous row, turn. *(30tr)*

Rep row 1 throughout, working 5 more rows in yarn A and 7 rows in yarn B.

Fasten off yarn.

76 Granny Stripes

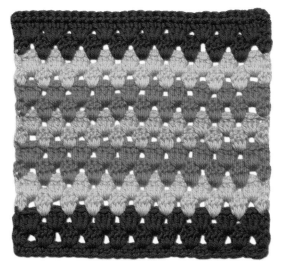

1 ☰
Ⓐ Ⓑ Ⓒ
Ⓓ

FOUNDATION CHAIN: Using yarn A, work 32ch.

FOUNDATION ROW: *(right side)* 1dc into 2nd ch from hook, 1dc into each ch to end, turn. *(31dc)*

ROW 1: 3ch *(counts as 1tr)*, 1tr into same place, [miss 2dc, 3tr into next dc] 9 times, miss 2dc, 2tr into next dc, turn.

ROW 2: 3ch *(counts as 1tr)*, [3tr into next sp between tr groups] 10 times, 1tr into 3rd of 3ch, turn. Break off yarn A.

ROW 3: Join yarn B, 3ch *(counts as 1tr)*, 1tr into same place, [3tr into next sp between tr groups] 9 times, 2tr into 3rd of 3ch, turn.

ROW 4: 3ch *(counts as 1tr)*, [3tr into next sp between tr groups] 10 times, 1tr into 3rd of 3ch, turn. Break off yarn B.

Rep rows 3 & 4 five times changing colour every two rows in the following colour sequence:
2 rows in yarn C, 2 rows in yarn D,

2 rows in yarn C, 2 rows in yarn B, 2 rows in yarn A.

NEXT ROW: 1ch, 1dc into each tr of previous row.

Fasten off yarn.

MIX-AND-MATCH

MIX-AND-MATCH

77 Raspberries & Cream

11

Special abbreviation

dc3tog = decrease 2 sts by working the next 3 dc together

FOUNDATION CHAIN: Using yarn A, work 58ch.

FOUNDATION ROW: *(wrong side)* 1dc into 2nd ch from hook, 1dc into each ch, turn. *(57dc)*

ROW 1: 1ch, 1dc into each of next 27dc, dc3tog, 1dc into each of rem 27dc, turn. *(55dc)*

ROW 2: 1ch, 1dc into each of next 26dc, dc3tog, 1dc into each of rem 26dc, turn. *(53dc)* Break off yarn A.

ROW 3: Join yarn B, 1ch, 1dc into each of next 25dc, dc3tog, 1dc into each of rem 25dc, turn. *(51dc)*

ROW 4: 1ch, 1dc into each of next 24dc, dc3tog, 1dc into each of rem 24dc, turn. *(49dc)* Break off yarn B.

Join yarn C. Cont in pattern as set, working dc3tog over 3 centre sts on every row. At the same time, change yarn colours in the following colour sequence:

Work 2 rows in yarn C, 2 rows in yarn D.

Join yarn E and cont in pattern until 3dc rem.

NEXT ROW: Work dc3tog.

Fasten off yarn.

MIX-AND-MATCH

78 Briar Rose

11

FOUNDATION RING: Using yarn A, work 6ch and join with ss to form a ring.

ROUND 1: 1ch, 16 dc into ring, join with ss into first dc. *(16dc)*

ROUND 2: 6ch *(counts as 1tr, 3ch)*, miss 2dc, [1tr into next dc, 3ch, miss 1dc] 7 times, join with ss into 3rd of 6ch. *(8 spaced tr)* Break off yarn A.

ROUND 3: Join yarn B to any 3ch sp, 1ch [1dc, 1htr, 1tr, 1htr, 1dc] into same sp, * [1dc, 1htr, 1tr, 1htr, 1dc] into next 3ch sp; rep from * 6 times, join with ss into first dc. *(8 petals made)*

ROUND 4: 1ch, 1dc into each dc and htr of previous round, working 3dc into each tr, join with ss into first dc. Break off yarn B.

ROUND 5: Join yarn C to 2nd dc of any petal, 1ch, 1dc into same place, * 5ch, miss 3dc, 1dc into next dc, 7ch, miss 2dc, 1dc into next dc, 5ch, miss 3dc, 1dc into next dc, 2ch, miss 2dc, ** 1dc into next dc; rep from * twice and from * to ** once again, join with ss into first dc.

ROUND 6: 2ch *(counts as 1htr)*, 3htr into next 5ch sp, * [4tr, 3ch, 4tr] into next 7ch sp, 4htr into next 5ch sp, 2htr into next 2ch sp, ** 4htr into next 5ch sp; rep from * twice and from * to ** once again, join with ss into 2nd of 2ch. Break off yarn C.

ROUND 7: Join yarn D to any 3ch corner sp, 3ch *(counts as 1tr)*, [1tr, 2ch, 2tr] into same sp, * 1tr into each of next 4tr, 1tr into each of next 3htr, 1ch, miss 1htr, 1tr into each of next 2htr, 1ch, miss 1htr, 1tr into each of next 3htr, 1tr into each of next 4tr, ** [2tr, 2ch, 2tr] into next 3ch corner sp; rep from * twice and from * to ** once again, join with ss into 3rd of 3ch.

ROUND 8: 3ch *(counts as 1tr)*, 1tr into next tr, * [2tr, 2ch, 2tr] into next 2ch corner sp, ** 1tr into each of next 20tr; rep from * twice and from * to ** once again, 1tr into each of next 18tr, join with ss into 3rd of 3ch.

ROUND 9: 1ch, 1dc into same place, 1dc into each tr of previous round, working 3dc into each 2ch corner sp, join with ss into first dc.

Fasten off yarn.

MIX-AND-MATCH

79 Baltic Square

11 📷 Ⓐ

Special abbreviations

beg pc = beginning popcorn made from 3ch and 4 tr sts, **pc** = popcorn made from 5 tr sts

FOUNDATION RING: Work 8ch and join with ss to form a ring.

ROUND 1: Beg pc into ring, [5ch, pc into ring] 3 times, 5ch, join with ss into top of beg pc.

ROUND 2: 3ch *(counts as 1tr)*, * [2tr, 2ch, pc, 2ch, 2tr] into next 5ch sp, ** 1tr into next pc; rep from * twice and from * to ** again, join with ss into 3rd of 3ch.

ROUND 3: 3ch *(counts as 1tr)*, 1tr into each of next 2 sts, * 2tr into next 2ch sp, 2ch, pc into next pc, 2ch, 2tr into next 2ch sp, ** 1tr into each of next 5tr, rep from * twice and from * to ** again, 1tr into each of last 2 sts, join with ss into 3rd of 3ch.

ROUND 4: 3ch *(counts as 1tr)*, 1tr into each of next 4tr, * 2tr into next 2ch sp, 3ch, pc into next pc, 3ch, 2tr into next 2ch sp, ** 1tr into each of next 9tr, rep from * twice and from * to ** again, 1tr into each of last 4tr, join with ss into 3rd of 3ch.

ROUND 5: 3ch *(counts as 1tr)*, 1tr into each of next 6tr, * 2tr into next 3ch sp, 3ch, pc into next pc, 3ch, 2tr into next 3ch sp, ** 1tr into each of next 13tr, rep from * twice and from * to ** again, 1tr into each of last 6tr, join with ss into 3rd of 3ch.

ROUND 6: 3ch *(counts as 1tr)*, 1tr into each of next 8tr, * 2tr into next 3ch sp, 3ch, pc into next pc, 3ch, 2tr into next 3ch sp, ** 1tr into each of next 17tr, rep from * twice and from * to ** again, 1tr into each of last 8tr, join with ss into 3rd of 3ch.

ROUND 7: 1ch, 1dc into each tr of previous round, working 3dc into each 3ch sp and [1htr, 1tr, 1htr] into top of each pc, join with ss into first dc.

Fasten off yarn.

80 Blocks & Shells

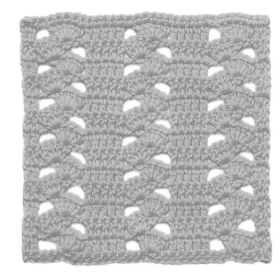

1 ▤

Ⓐ

FOUNDATION CHAIN: Work 33ch.

FOUNDATION ROW: *(wrong side)* 1dc into 2nd ch from hook, 1dc into each ch, turn. *(32dc)*

ROW 1: 3ch *(counts as 1tr)*, 1tr into next dc, * miss 2dc, 5tr into next dc, 2ch, miss 3dc, 1tr into each of next 5dc; rep from * ending last rep 1tr into each of last 2dc, turn.

ROW 2: 3ch *(counts as 1tr)*, 1tr into next tr, * miss 2ch, 5tr into next tr, 2ch, miss 4tr, 1tr into each of next 5tr; rep from * ending last rep 1tr into each of last 2tr, turn.

Rep row 2 11 times.

NEXT ROW: 1ch, 1dc into each tr of previous row, working 1dc into each 2ch sp.

Fasten off yarn.

MIX-AND-MATCH

 33 83 111

MIX-AND-MATCH

 36 97 98

81 Sunshine & Showers

FOUNDATION RING: Using yarn A, work 4ch and join with ss to form a ring.

ROUND 1: 1ch, [1dc into ring, 3ch] 8 times, join with ss into first dc. Break off yarn A.

ROUND 2: Join yarn B to any 3ch sp, 3ch *(counts as 1tr)*, [1tr, 2ch, 2tr] into same sp, * 2tr into next 3ch sp, ** [2tr, 2ch, 2tr] into next 3ch sp; rep from * twice and from * to ** once again, join with ss into 3rd of 3ch. Break off yarn B.

ROUND 3: Join yarn C to any 2ch corner sp, 3ch *(counts as 1tr)*, [2tr, 3ch, 3tr] into same sp,* [2tr in sp between next two 2tr groups] twice, ** [3tr, 3ch, 3tr] into next 2ch corner sp; rep from * twice and from * to ** once again, join with ss into 3rd of 3ch.

ROUND 4: 1ch, 1dc into same place, 1dc into each tr of previous round, working 3dc into each 3ch corner sp, join with ss into first dc. Break off yarn C.

ROUND 5: Join yarn D, 3ch *(counts as 1tr)*, 1tr into each dc of previous round, working [2tr, 2ch, 2tr] into centre st of each 3dc corner group, join with ss into 3rd of 3ch.

ROUND 6: 1ch, 1dc into same place, 1dc into each tr of previous round, working 3dc into each 2ch corner sp, join with ss into first dc. Break off yarn D.

ROUND 7: Join yarn C, 3ch *(counts as 1tr)*, 1tr into each dc of previous round, working [2tr, 2ch, 2tr] into centre st of each 3dc corner group, join with ss into 3rd of 3ch.

ROUND 8: 1ch, 1dc into same place, 1dc into each tr of previous round, working 3dc into each 2ch corner sp, join with ss into first dc. Break off yarn C.

ROUNDS 9 & 10: Join yarn B, 1ch, 1dc into same place, 1dc into each dc of previous round, working 3dc into centre st of each 3dc corner group, join with ss into first dc.

Fasten off yarn.

MIX-AND-MATCH

 23 56 206

82 Webbed Lace

FOUNDATION CHAIN: Work 33ch.

FOUNDATION ROW: *(right side)* 1tr into 4th ch from hook, 1tr into each ch to end, turn. *(31tr)*

ROW 1: 3ch *(counts as 1tr)*, 1tr into each tr of previous row, turn. *(31tr)*

ROW 2: 3ch *(counts as 1tr)*, 1tr into each of next 4tr, * 4ch, [miss 1tr, 1dtr into next tr] 4 times, 4ch, miss 1tr, 1tr into each of next 3tr; rep from * once, 1tr into next tr, 1tr into 3rd of 3ch, turn.

ROWS 3 & 4: 3ch *(counts as 1tr)*, 1tr into each of next 4tr, * 4ch, 1dc into each of next 4dtr, 4ch, 1tr into each of next 3tr; rep from * once, 1tr into next tr, 1tr into 3rd of 3ch, turn.

ROW 5: 3ch *(counts as 1tr)*, 1tr into each of next 4tr, * [1ch, 1dtr into next dc] 4 times, 1ch, 1tr into each of next 3tr; rep from * once, 1tr into next tr, 1tr into 3rd of 3ch, turn.

ROW 6: 3ch *(counts as 1tr)*, 1tr into each of next 4tr, * [1tr into 1ch sp, 1tr into next dtr] 4 times, 1tr into next 1ch sp, 1tr into each of next 3tr; rep from * once, 1tr into next tr, 1tr into 3rd of 3ch, turn. *(31tr)*

Rep rows 1 to 6, then rep row 1 once again.

Fasten off yarn.

MIX-AND-MATCH

 21 54 210

83 Diamond in a Square

11 A B C

FOUNDATION RING: Using yarn A, work 4ch and join with ss to form a ring.

ROUND 1: 6ch *(counts as 1tr, 3ch)*, [3tr into ring, 3ch] 3 times, 2tr into ring, join with ss into 3rd of 6ch.

ROUND 2: Ss into next 3ch sp, 3ch *(counts as 1tr)*, [2tr, 2ch, 3tr] into same sp, * 1tr into each of next 3tr, [3tr, 2ch, 3tr] into next 3ch sp; rep from * twice, 1tr into each of next 3tr, join with ss into 3rd of 3ch. Break off yarn A.

ROUND 3: Join yarn B to any 2ch sp, * 6ch, miss 4tr, 1dtr into next tr, 6ch, ss into next 2ch sp; rep from * 3 times, join with ss into first ch.

ROUND 4: 1ch, * 7dc into next 6ch sp, [1htr, 2ch, 1htr] into next dtr to make corner, 7dc into next 6ch sp, 1dc into 2ch sp of round 2; rep from * 3 times, join with ss into first dc.

ROUND 5: 2ch *(counts as 1htr)*, 1htr into each of next 6dc, 1tr into next htr, * [2tr, 2ch, 2tr] into next 2ch corner sp, 1tr into next htr, 1htr into each of next 7dc, 1tr into next dc, ** 1htr into each of next 7dc; rep from * twice and from * to ** once again,

join with ss into 2nd of 2ch. Break off yarn B.

ROUND 6: Join yarn C into centre tr along one side of square, 3ch *(counts as 1tr)*, * 1tr into each of next 7htr, 1htr into each of next 3tr, [2htr, 2ch, 2htr] into next 2ch corner sp, 1htr into each of next 3tr, 1tr into next tr; rep from * 3 times, join with ss into 3rd of 3ch. Break off yarn C.

ROUND 7: Join yarn A to any st along one side of square, 1ch, 1dc into same place, 1dc into each htr and tr of previous round, working 3dc into each 2ch corner sp, join with ss into first dc.

ROUND 8: 1ch, 1dc into same place, 1dc into each dc of previous round, working 3dc into centre st of each 3dc corner group, join with ss into first dc.

Fasten off yarn.

MIX-AND-MATCH

84 Combination Stripes

11 A B C D E

FOUNDATION CHAIN: Using yarn A, work 2ch.

FOUNDATION ROW: *(right side)* Work 5dc into 2nd ch from hook, turn. *(5dc)*

ROW 1: 1ch, 1dc into each of next 2dc, [1dc, 2ch, 1dc] into next dc *(centre st)*, 1dc into each of next 2dc, turn.

ROW 2: 1ch, 1dc into each of next 3dc, [1dc, 2ch, 1dc] into 2ch corner sp, 1dc into each of next 3dc, turn.

ROW 3: 1ch, 1dc into each of next 4dc, [1dc, 2ch, 1dc] into 2ch corner sp, 1dc into each of next 4dc, turn.

Cont in pattern as set, working 1 more dc at each side of corner until 4 more rows have been worked in A. Break off yarn A.

Join yarn B and work 2 rows. Break off yarn B.

Join yarn C and work 2 rows. Break off yarn C.

Join yarn D and work 2 rows. Break off yarn D.

Join yarn E and work 2 rows. Break off yarn E.

ROW 16: Join yarn A, 3ch *(counts as 1tr)*, 1tr into each of next 16dc, [2tr,

2ch, 2tr] into 2ch corner sp, 1tr into each of next 17dc, turn.

ROW 17: 3ch *(counts as 1tr)*, 1tr into each of next 18tr, [2tr, 2ch, 2tr] into 2ch corner sp, 1tr into each of next 19tr, turn.

ROW 18: 3ch *(counts as 1tr)*, 1tr into each of next 20tr, [2tr, 2ch, 2tr] into 2ch corner sp, 1tr into each of next 21tr, turn.

ROW 19: 3ch *(counts as 1tr)*, 1tr into each of next 22tr, [2tr, 2ch, 2tr] into 2ch corner sp, 1tr into each of next 23tr, turn. Break off yarn A.

ROW 20: Join yarn B, 1ch, 1dc into first tr, 1dc into each of next 24tr, [1dc, 2ch, 1dc] into 2ch corner sp, 1dc into each of next 25tr, turn.

ROW 21: 1ch, 1dc into each of next 26dc, [1dc, 2ch, 1dc] into 2ch corner sp, 1dc into each of next 26dc, turn. Break off yarn B.

ROW 22: Join yarn C, 1ch, 1dc into each of next 27dc, [1dc, 2ch, 1dc] into 2ch corner sp, 1dc into each of next 27dc, turn.

ROW 23: 1ch, 1dc into each of next 28dc, 3dc into 2ch corner sp, 1dc into each of next 28dc.

Fasten off yarn.

MIX-AND-MATCH

85 Lemon Stripe

11 A B

Special abbreviations

beg pc = beginning popcorn made from 3ch and 4 tr sts, **pc** = popcorn made from 5 tr sts

FOUNDATION RING: Using yarn A, work 6ch and join with ss to form a ring.

ROUND 1: 3ch *(counts as 1tr)*, [1tr, pc, 2tr] into ring, 2ch, * [2tr, pc, 2tr] into ring, 2ch; rep from * twice, join with ss into 3rd of 3ch.

ROUND 2: 3ch *(counts as 1tr)*, 1tr into each of next 4 sts, [1tr, 3ch, 1tr] into next 2ch sp *(corner made)*, * 1tr into each of next 5 sts, [1tr, 3ch, 1tr] into next 2ch sp *(corner made)*; rep from * twice, join with ss into 3rd of 3ch.

ROUND 3: 3ch *(counts as 1tr)*, pc into next tr, 1tr into next tr, pc into next tr, 1tr into each of next 2tr, * [1tr, 3ch, 1tr] into next 3ch corner sp, ** 1tr into each of next 2tr, pc into next tr, 1tr into next tr, pc into next tr, 1tr into each of next 2tr; rep from * twice and from * to ** once again, 1tr into next tr, join with ss into 3rd of 3ch.

ROUND 4: 3ch *(counts as 1tr)*, 1tr into each of next 6 sts, [1tr, 4ch, 1tr] into next 3ch corner sp, * 1tr into each of next 9 sts, [1tr, 4ch, 1tr] into next 3ch corner sp; rep from * twice, 1tr into each of next 2 sts, join with ss into 3rd of 3ch.

ROUND 5: Beg pc into same ch, 1tr into each of next 3tr, pc into next tr, 1tr into each of next 3tr, * [1tr, 3ch, 1tr] into next 4ch corner sp, ** 1tr into each of next 3tr, [pc into next tr, 1tr into each of next 3tr] twice; rep from * twice and from * to ** once again, 1tr into each of next 3tr, join with ss into 3rd of 3ch. Break off yarn A.

ROUND 6: Join yarn B, 3ch *(counts as 1tr)*, 1tr into each of next 8 sts, * [3tr, 3ch, 3tr] into next 4ch corner sp, ** 1tr into each of next 13 sts; rep from * twice and from * to ** once again, 1tr into each of next 4 sts, join with ss into 3rd of 3ch. Break off yarn B.

ROUND 7: Join yarn A, 3ch *(counts as 1tr)*, 1tr into each of next 11tr, * 5tr into next 3ch corner sp, ** 1tr into each of next 19tr; rep from * twice and from * to ** once again, 1tr into each of next 7tr, join with ss into 3rd of 3ch.

Fasten off yarn.

MIX-AND-MATCH

 30 156 199

86 Sunray

11 A B

FOUNDATION RING: Using yarn A, work 6ch and join with ss to form a ring.

ROUND 1: 4ch *(counts as 1dtr)*, 1dtr into ring, 2ch, [2dtr into ring, 2ch] 7 times, join with ss into 4th of 4ch.

ROUND 2: 3ch *(counts as 1tr)*, 2tr into next dtr, 2ch, [1tr into next dtr, 2tr into next dtr, 2ch] 7 times, join with ss into 3rd of 3ch.

ROUND 3: 3ch *(counts as 1tr)*, 3tr into next tr, 1tr into next tr, 2ch, * 1tr into next tr, 3tr into next tr, 1tr into next tr, 2ch; rep from * 6 times, join with ss into 3rd of 3ch.

ROUND 4: 3ch *(counts as 1tr)*, 2htr into next tr, 1dc into each of next 3tr, 1dc into next 2ch sp, 1dc into each of next 3tr, 2htr into next tr, 1tr into next tr, * 3ch *(corner sp made)*, 1tr into next tr, 2htr into next tr, 1dc into each of next 3tr, 1dc into next 2ch sp, 1dc into each of next 3tr, 2htr into next tr, 1tr into next tr; rep from * twice, 3ch *(corner sp made)*, join with ss into 3rd of 3ch.

ROUND 5: 3ch *(counts as 1tr)*, 2tr into same place, * 1htr into each of next 5 sts, miss 1 st, 2ch, 1htr into each of next 5 sts, 3tr into next st, 3ch, ** 3tr into next st; rep from * twice and from * to ** once again, join with ss into 3rd of 3ch.

ROUND 6: 3ch *(counts as 1tr)*, 1tr into each of next 7 sts, * 2tr into next 2ch sp, 1tr into each of next 8 sts, 5tr into next 3ch corner sp, ** 1tr into each of next 8 sts; rep from * twice and from * to ** once again, join with ss into 3rd of 3ch. Break off yarn A.

ROUND 7: Join yarn B to any tr along side of square, 2ch *(counts as 1htr)*, 1htr into each tr of previous round, working 3htr into centre st of each 5tr corner group, join with ss into 2nd of 2ch.

Fasten off yarn.

MIX-AND-MATCH

 125 185 197

87 Peony

FOUNDATION CHAIN: Using yarn A, work 2ch.

FOUNDATION RING: Work 8dc into 2nd ch from hook, join with ss into first dc. Break off yarn A.

ROUND 1: Join yarn B to any dc, 1ch, 1dc into same place, 2ch, [1dc into next dc, 2ch] 7 times, join with ss into first dc.

ROUND 2: Ss into first 2ch sp, 1ch, [1dc, 1htr, 1dc] into same sp, [1dc, 1htr, 1dc] into next 2ch sp 7 times, join with ss into back of first dc. *(8 petals made)*

ROUND 3: Working behind petals, [3ch, ss behind first dc of next petal] 7 times, 3ch, join with ss into first of 3ch.

ROUND 4: Working behind petals, ss into first 3ch sp, 1ch, [1dc, 3htr, 1dc] into same sp, [1dc, 3htr, 1dc] into next 3ch sp 7 times, join with ss into back of first dc. *(8 petals made)*

ROUND 5: Working behind petals, [5ch, ss behind first dc of next petal] 7 times, 5ch, join with ss into first of 3ch.

ROUND 6: Working behind petals, ss into first 5ch sp, 1ch, [1dc, 2htr, 3tr, 2htr, 1dc] into same sp, [1dc, 2htr, 3tr, 2htr, 1dc] into next 5ch sp 7 times, join with ss into back of first dc. *(8 petals made)*

ROUND 7: Working behind petals, [6ch, ss behind first dc of next petal] 7 times, 6ch, join with ss into first of 3ch.

ROUND 8: Working behind petals, ss into first 6ch sp, 1ch, [1dc, 2htr, 5tr, 2htr, 1dc] into same sp, [1dc, 2htr, 5tr, 2htr, 1dc] into next 6ch sp 7 times, join with ss into back of first dc. *(8 petals made)* Break off yarn B.

ROUND 9: Working behind petals, join yarn C to back of first dc on any petal, [8ch, ss behind first dc of next petal] 7 times, 8ch, join with ss into first of 3ch.

ROUND 10: Ss into next 8ch sp, 1ch, 8dc into same sp, * [4tr, 2ch, 4tr] into next 8ch sp *(corner made)*, ** 8dc into next 8ch sp; rep from * twice and from * to ** once again, join with ss into first dc.

ROUND 11: 3ch *(counts as 1tr)*, 1tr into each dc and tr of previous round, working [2tr, 2ch, 2tr] into each 2ch corner sp, join with ss into 3rd of 3ch.

ROUND 12: 1ch, 1dc into same place, 1dc into each tr of previous round, working 3dc into each 2ch corner sp, join with ss into first dc. Break off yarn C.

ROUND 13: Join yarn B to any dc along side of square, 1ch, 1dc into each dc of previous round, working 3dc into centre st of each 3dc corner group, join with ss into first dc.

ROUNDS 14 & 15: 1ch, 1dc into each dc of previous round, working 3dc into centre st of each 3dc corner group, join with ss into first dc.

Fasten off yarn.

MIX-AND-MATCH

88 Edwardian Fancy

FOUNDATION RING: Using yarn A, work 4ch and join with ss to form a ring.

ROUND 1: 3ch *(counts as 1tr)*, 11tr into ring, join with ss into 3rd of 3ch. *(12tr)* Break off yarn A.

ROUND 2: Join yarn B to any dc, 5ch *(counts as 1tr, 2ch)*, * 1tr into next dc, 2ch; rep from * 10 times, join with ss into 3rd of 5ch. *(12 spaced tr)*

ROUND 3: Ss into next 2ch sp, 1ch, 3dc into same sp, * 3dc into next 2ch sp; rep from * to end, join with ss into first dc. Break off yarn B.

ROUND 4: Join yarn C to last st of any 3dc group, 1ch, 1dc into same place, 1dc into next dc, * 2dc into next dc, 1dc into each of next 2dc; rep from * 10 times, 2dc into next dc, join with ss into first dc.

ROUND 5: 1ch, [1dc, 1tr] into same place, 1ch, [1tr, 1dc] into next dc, * ss into each of next 2dc, [1dc, 1tr] into next dc, 1ch, [1tr, 1dc] into next dc; rep from * 10 times, ss into next 2dc, join with ss into first dc.

ROUND 6: Ss into next 1ch sp, 1ch, 1dc into same sp, 5ch, * 1dc into next 1ch sp, 5ch; rep from * 10 times, join with ss into first dc.

ROUND 7: Ss into next 5ch sp, 1ch, [1dc, 1htr, 2tr, 2ch, 2tr, 1htr, 1dc] into same sp *(corner made)*, * 1dc into next dc, [4dc into next 5ch sp, 1dc into next dc] twice, ** [1dc, 1htr, 2tr, 2ch, 2tr, 1htr, 1dc] into next 5ch sp *(corner made)*; rep from * twice and from * to ** once again, join with ss into first dc.

ROUND 8: 1ch, 1dc into each st of previous round, working 3dc into each 2ch corner sp, join with ss into first dc. Break off yarn C.

ROUND 9: Join yarn D to centre st of any 3dc corner group, 3ch *(counts as 1tr)*, [1tr, 2ch, 2tr] into same place, * 1tr into next dc, 1ch, miss 1dc, [1tr into next dc, 1ch, miss 1dc] 9 times, 1tr into next dc, ** [2tr, 2ch, 2tr] into next dc; rep from * twice and from * to ** once again, join with ss into 3rd of 3ch. Break off yarn D.

ROUND 10: Join yarn A to any tr along side of square, 1ch, 1dc into each tr and ch of previous round, working 3dc into each 2ch corner sp, join with ss into first dc. Break off yarn A.

ROUND 11: Join yarn D to any dc along side of square, 1ch, 1dc into each dc of previous round, working 3dc into centre st of each 3dc corner group, join with ss into first dc. Break off yarn A.

Fasten off yarn.

MIX-AND-MATCH

89 Spinner

11
Ⓐ Ⓑ Ⓒ

FOUNDATION RING: Using yarn A, work 4ch and join with ss to form a ring.

ROUND 1: 3ch (counts as 1tr), 15tr into ring, join with ss into 3rd of 3ch. (16 tr) Break off yarn A.

ROUND 2: Join yarn B into sp between any 2tr, 3ch (counts as 1tr), 1tr into same sp, 2tr into each rem sp between tr, join with ss into 3rd of 3ch. (32tr)

ROUND 3: 3ch (counts as 1tr), 1tr into same place, 1tr into next tr, [2tr into next tr, 1tr into next tr] 15 times, join with ss into 3rd of 3ch. (48tr) Break off yarn B.

ROUND 4: Join yarn C to any tr, 4ch (counts as 1dtr), [2tr, 2ch, 2tr, 1dtr] into same place, * miss next 2tr, 1htr into each of next 2tr, 1dc into each of next 3tr, 1htr into each of next 2tr, miss next 2tr, ** [1dtr, 2tr, 2ch, 2tr, 1dtr] into next tr; rep from * twice and from * to ** once again, join with ss into 4th of 4ch. Break off yarn C.

ROUND 5: Join yarn A to any 2ch corner sp, 3ch (counts as 1tr), [2dtr, 2ch, 2dtr, 1tr] into same sp, * 1tr into each st along side of square, ** [1tr, 2dtr, 2ch, 2dtr, 1tr] into next 2ch corner sp; rep from * twice and from * to ** once again, join with ss into 3rd of 3ch. Break off yarn A.

ROUND 6: Join yarn B to any 2ch corner sp, 3ch (counts as 1tr), [1tr, 2ch, 2tr] into same sp, * 1tr into each st along side of square, ** [2tr, 2ch, 2tr into next 2ch corner sp; rep from * twice and from * to ** once again, join with ss into 3rd of 3ch.

ROUND 7: 3ch (counts as 1tr), 1tr into each tr of previous round, working 5tr into each 2ch corner sp, join with ss into 3rd of 3ch.

Fasten off yarn.

MIX-AND-MATCH

 10   117   173

90 Bright Triangles

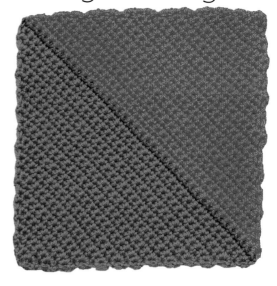

11
Ⓐ Ⓑ

Special abbreviation

dc3tog = decrease 2 sts by working the next 3 dc together

FOUNDATION CHAIN: Using yarn A, work 2ch.

FOUNDATION ROW: (wrong side) Work 3dc into 2nd ch from hook, turn. (3dc)

ROW 1: 1ch, 2dc into first dc, 1dc into next dc, 2dc into last dc, turn. (5dc) Begin increase pattern.

ROWS 2 to 4: 1ch, 2dc into first dc, 1dc into each dc along row to last st, 2dc into last dc, turn.

ROW 5: 1ch, 1dc into each dc along row, turn.

Rep rows 2 to 5 five times. (41dc) Break off yarn A.

Join yarn B and begin decrease pattern.

NEXT ROW: 1ch, 1dc into each dc along row, turn.

NEXT 3 ROWS: 1ch, miss first dc, 1dc into each dc along row to last 2 sts, miss 1 dc, 1dc into last dc, turn.

Rep four-row decrease pattern five times. (5dc)

NEXT ROW: 1ch, miss first dc, 1dc into each of next 2dc, miss next dc, 1dc into next dc, turn. (3dc)

NEXT ROW: 1ch, work dc3tog.

Fasten off yarn.

MIX-AND-MATCH

 59   132   172

91 Terraces

111
A B C
D E

FOUNDATION CHAIN: Using yarn A, work 31ch.

FOUNDATION ROW: (right side) 1dc into 2nd ch from hook, 1dc into each ch, turn. (30dc)

ROW 1: 1ch, 1dc into each dc, turn. Break off yarn A.

ROW 2: Join yarn B, 3ch (counts as 1tr), miss first dc, 1tr into next dc, * 2ch, miss 2dc, 1tr into each of next 2dc; rep from * to end, turn.

ROW 3: 1ch, 1dc into each of next 2tr, * 2ch, 1dc into each of next 2tr; rep from * to end, turn. Break off yarn B.

ROW 4: Join yarn C, 1ch, 1dc into each of first 2dc, * 1dtr into each of next 2 missed dc 3 rows below, 1dc into each of next 2dc; rep from * to end, turn.

ROW 5: 1ch, 1dc into each dc and dtr of previous row, turn. Break off yarn C.

ROW 6: Join yarn A, 3ch (counts as 1tr), 1tr into each dc of previous row, turn.

ROW 7: 1ch, 1dc into each tr of previous row, turn. Break off yarn A.
Join yarn D and rep rows 2 & 3. Break off yarn D.
Join yarn E and rep rows 4 & 5. Break off yarn E.
Join yarn A and rep rows 6 & 7. Break off yarn A.
Join yarn C and rep rows 2 & 3. Break off yarn C.
Join yarn B and rep rows 4 & 5. Break off yarn B.
Join yarn A and rep rows 6 & 7. Break off yarn A.
Join yarn E and rep rows 2 & 3. Break off yarn E.
Join yarn D and rep rows 4 & 5. Break off yarn D.
Join yarn A and rep row 1 twice.
Fasten off yarn

MIX-AND-MATCH

 47
 104
 121

92 Victorian Lace

11 📷 A

Special abbreviations

dtr2tog = work 2dtr together, **beg cl** = beginning cluster made from 2 tr sts, **cl** = cluster made from 3 tr sts

FOUNDATION RING: Work 10ch and join with ss to form a ring.

ROUND 1: 4ch (counts as 1dtr), 1tr into ring, 2ch, [dtr2tog into ring, 2ch] 11 times, join with ss into 4th of 4ch.

ROUND 2: Ss into next 2ch sp, 3ch (counts as 1tr), beg cl into same sp, 3ch, [cl into next 2ch sp, 3ch] 11 times, join with ss into top of beg cl.

ROUND 3: 5ch (counts as 1htr, 3ch), miss next 3ch sp, [cl, 2ch, cl, 4ch, cl, 2ch, cl] into next 3ch sp, 3ch, * miss next 3ch sp, 1htr into top of next cl, 3ch, miss next 3ch sp, [cl, 2ch, cl, 4ch, cl, 2ch, cl] into next 3ch sp, 3ch; rep from * twice, join with ss into 2nd of 5ch.

ROUND 4: Ss into next 3ch sp, 4ch (counts as 1tr, 1ch), 1tr into same sp, * 1ch, 1tr into top of next cl, 1ch, 1tr into next 2ch sp, 1ch, [cl, 2ch, cl, 4ch, cl, 2ch, cl] into next 4ch sp, 1ch, 1tr into next 2ch sp, 1ch, 1tr into top of next cl, 1ch, 1tr into next 3ch sp, 1ch,

** 1tr into next htr, 1ch, 1tr into next 3ch sp; rep from * twice and from * to ** once again, join with ss into 3rd of 4ch.

ROUND 5: 4ch (counts as 1tr, 2ch), [1tr into next tr, 1ch] 3 times, * 1tr into top of next cl, 1ch, 1tr into next 2ch sp, 1ch, [cl, 2ch, cl, 4ch, cl, 2ch, cl] into next 4ch corner sp, 1ch, 1tr into next 2ch sp, 1ch, 1tr into top of next cl, 1ch, ** [1tr into next tr, 1ch] 7 times; rep from * twice and from * to ** once again, [1tr into next tr, 1ch] 3 times, join with ss into 3rd of 4ch.

ROUND 6: 4ch (counts as 1tr, 1ch), [1tr into next tr, 1ch] 5 times, * 1tr into top of next cl, 1ch, 1tr into next 2ch sp, 1ch, 5tr into next 4ch corner sp, 1ch, 1tr into next 2ch sp, 1ch, 1tr into top of next cl, 1ch, ** [1tr into next tr, 1ch] 11 times; rep from * twice and from * to ** once again, [1tr into next tr, 1ch] 5 times, join with ss into 3rd of 4ch.

Fasten off yarn.

MIX-AND-MATCH

 9
 57
 192

93 Sequenced Stripes

1 ▤

Ⓐ Ⓑ Ⓒ
Ⓓ Ⓔ

FOUNDATION CHAIN: Using yarn A, work 30ch.

FOUNDATION ROW: *(right side)* 1dc into 2nd ch from hook, 1dc into each ch to end, turn. *(29dc)*

ROW 1: 1ch, 1dc into each st of previous row, turn. *(29dc)*

ROWS 2, 3, 4 & 5: Rep row 1. Break off yarn A.

ROW 6: Join yarn B, 1ch, 1dc into each of next 2dc, * 1ch, miss 1dc, 1dc into next dc; rep from * to last 3 sts, 1ch, miss 1dc, 1ch into each of next 2dc, turn.

ROW 7: 1ch, 1dc into each dc and 1 ch sp of previous row, turn. *(29dc)* Break off yarn B.

Rep rows 6 and 7 11 more times, changing yarn colour every two rows and using the following sequence:

C, D, E, A, B, A, E, D, C, B, A.

Cont with yarn A and rep row 1 three times.

Fasten off yarn.

MIX-AND-MATCH

94 Gothic Square

11 ⟲ Ⓐ Ⓑ Ⓒ Ⓓ

Special abbreviations

beg cl = beginning cluster of tr2tog,
cl = cluster of tr3tog

FOUNDATION RING: Using yarn A, work 4ch and join with ss to form a ring.

ROUND 1: 4ch *(counts as 1tr, 1ch)*, [1tr into ring, 1ch] 11 times, join with ss into 3rd of 4ch. *(12 spaced tr)* Break off yarn A.

ROUND 2: Join yarn B to any 1ch sp, 3ch *(counts as 1tr)*, beg cl in same sp, [3ch, cl into next 1ch sp] 11 times, 3ch, join with ss into top of beg cl.

ROUND 3: Ss into centre st of next 3ch sp, 1ch, 1dc into same sp, [5ch, 1dc into next 3ch sp] 11 times, join with ss into first dc. Break off yarn B.

ROUND 4: Join yarn C to centre st of any 5ch sp, 3ch *(counts as 1tr)*, 4tr into same sp, * 1ch, 1dc into next 5ch sp, 5ch, 1dc into next 5ch sp, 1ch, ** [5tr, 3ch, 5tr] into next 5ch sp; rep from * twice and from * to ** once again, 5tr into next 5ch sp, 3ch, join with ss into 3rd of 3ch. Break off yarn C.

ROUND 5: Join yarn D to any 3ch sp, 3ch *(counts as 1tr)*, [1tr, 2ch, 2tr] into same sp, * 1tr into each of next 4tr, 4ch, 1dc into next 5ch sp, 4ch, miss next tr, 1tr into each of next 4tr, ** [2tr, 2ch, 2tr] into next 3ch sp; rep from * twice and from * to ** once again, join with ss into 3rd of 3ch.

ROUND 6: Ss in next tr and into next 2ch sp, 3ch *(counts as 1tr)*, [1tr, 2ch, 2tr] into same sp, * 1tr into each of next 4tr, [4ch, 1dc into next 4ch sp] twice, 4ch, miss next 2tr, 1tr into each of next 4tr, ** [2tr, 2ch, 2tr] into next 2ch sp; rep from * twice and from * to ** once again, join with ss into 3rd of 3ch.

ROUND 7: 3ch *(counts as 1tr)*, 1tr into next tr, * 5tr into next 2ch corner sp, 1tr into each of next 6tr, 4tr into next 4ch sp, 3tr into next 4ch sp, 4tr into next 4ch sp, ** 1tr into each of next 6tr; rep from * twice and from * to ** once again, 1tr into each of next 4tr, join with ss into 3rd of 3ch. Fasten off yarn.

MIX-AND-MATCH

95 Kingcup

111 Ⓐ Ⓑ Ⓒ

Special abbreviation

bpdc = back post double crochet

FOUNDATION RING: Using yarn A, work 6ch and join with ss to form a ring.

ROUND 1: 3ch (counts as 1tr), 11tr into ring, join with ss into 3rd of 3ch. (12 tr)

ROUND 2: 2ch (counts as 1htr), 1htr into same place, 2htr into each of next 11tr, join with ss into 2nd of 2ch. (24htr)

ROUND 3: 1ch, 1dc into same place, * 5ch, miss next 2htr, 1dc into next htr; rep from * 6 times, 5ch, join with ss into first dc. Break off yarn A.

ROUND 4: Join yarn B to any 5ch sp, 1ch, [1dc, 1htr, 5tr, 1htr, 1dc] into same 5ch sp (petal made), [1dc, 1htr, 5tr, 1htr, 1dc] into next 5ch sp 7 times, join with ss into back loop of first dc. (8 petals)

ROUND 5: Working behind petals of previous round, [5ch, bpdc round next dc] 8 times, do not join round. (8 5ch sps)

ROUND 6: Ss into next 5ch sp, [1dc, 1htr, 7tr, 1htr, 1dc] into same 5ch sp

(petal made), [1dc, 1htr, 7tr, 1htr, 1dc] into next 5ch sp 7 times, join with ss into back loop of first dc. Break off yarn B.

ROUND 7: Join yarn C to 3rd tr of any petal of previous round, 1ch, 1dc into same place, 1dc into each of next 2tr, * 5ch, 1dc into each of centre 3tr of next petal, 8ch, ** 1dc into each of centre 3tr of next petal; rep from * twice and from * to ** once again, join with ss into first dc.

ROUND 8: 3ch (counts as 1tr), 1tr into each dc of previous round, working 5tr into each 5ch sp and [5tr, 3ch, 5tr] into each 8ch sp to make corner, join with ss into 3rd of 3ch.

ROUND 9: 3ch (counts as 1tr), 1tr into each tr of previous round, working [2tr, 2ch, 2tr] into each 3ch corner sp, join with ss into 3rd of 3ch. Break off yarn C.

ROUND 10: Join yarn B, 1ch, 1dc into same place, 1dc into each tr of previous round, working 3dc into each 2ch corner sp, join with ss into first dc.

Fasten off yarn.

MIX-AND-MATCH

 38   47   165

96 Light & Shade

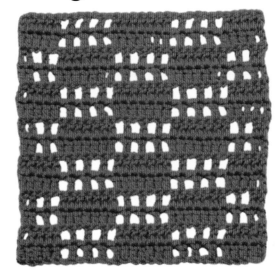

11 Ⓐ

FOUNDATION CHAIN: Work 33ch.

FOUNDATION ROW: (right side) 1tr into 4th ch from hook, 1tr into each of next 2ch, [1tr into next ch, 1ch, miss 1ch] 4 times, 1tr into each of next 6ch, [1tr into next ch, 1ch, miss 1ch] 4 times, 1tr into each of next 5ch, turn.

ROW 1: 3ch (counts as 1tr), 1tr into each of next 3tr, [1tr into next tr, 1ch, miss 1tr] 4 times, 1tr into each of next 6tr, [1tr into next tr, 1ch, miss 1tr] 4 times, 1tr into each of next 5tr, turn.

ROWS 2 & 3: 3ch (counts as 1tr), [1tr into next tr, 1ch, miss 1tr] twice, 1tr into each of next 6tr, [1tr into next tr, 1ch, miss 1tr] 4 times, 1tr into each of next 6tr, [1tr into next tr, 1ch, miss 1tr] twice, 1tr into each of next 2tr, turn.

ROWS 4 & 5: 3ch (counts as 1tr), 1tr into each of next 3tr, [1tr into next tr, 1ch, miss 1tr] 4 times, 1tr into each of next 6tr, [1tr into next tr,

1ch, miss 1tr] 4 times, 1tr into each of next 5tr, turn.

Rep rows 2 to 5 twice.

Fasten off yarn.

MIX-AND-MATCH

 48   166   190

97 Eyelet Lace

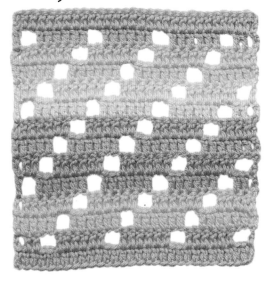

1

A B C
D E

98 Old Vienna

1

A

FOUNDATION CHAIN: Using yarn A, work 32ch

FOUNDATION ROW: *(right side)* 1tr into 4th ch from hook, 1tr into each ch to end, turn. *(30tr)*

ROW 1: 3ch *(counts as 1tr)*, 1tr into each of next 2tr, * 2ch, miss 2tr, 1tr into each of next 6tr; rep from * twice, 2ch, miss 2tr, 1tr into 3rd of 3ch, turn. Break off yarn A.

ROW 2: Join yarn B, 3ch *(counts as 1tr)*, * 1tr into each of next 2ch, 1tr into each of next 4tr, 2ch, miss 2tr; rep from * twice, 1tr into each of next 2ch, 1tr into each of next 2tr, 1tr into 3rd of 3ch, turn.

ROW 3: 3ch *(counts as 1tr)*, * 1tr into each of next 4tr, 1tr into each of next 2ch, 2ch, miss 2tr; rep from * twice, 1tr into each of next 4tr, 1tr into 3rd of 3ch, turn. Break off yarn B.

ROW 4: Join yarn C, 3ch *(counts as 1tr)*, 1tr into each of next 2tr, * 2ch, miss 2tr, 1tr into each of next 2ch, 1tr into each of next 4tr; rep from *

twice, 2ch, miss 2tr, 1tr into 3rd of 3ch, turn. Break off yarn A.

ROW 5: Rep row 1. Break off yarn C.

ROW 6: Join yarn D, rep row 2.

ROW 7: Rep row 3. Break off yarn D.

ROW 8: Join yarn E, rep row 4.

ROW 9: Rep row 1. Break off yarn E.

ROW 10: Join yarn B, rep row 2.

ROW 11: Rep row 3. Break off yarn B.

ROW 12: Join yarn A, rep row 4.

ROW 13: 3ch *(counts as 1tr)*, 1tr into each tr and ch of previous row. *(30tr)*

Fasten off yarn

MIX-AND-MATCH

 121 162 194

FOUNDATION RING: Work 8ch and join with ss to form a ring.

ROUND 1: 3ch *(counts as 1tr)*, 2tr into ring, 5ch, * 3tr into ring, 5ch; rep from * twice, join with ss into 3rd of 3ch.

ROUND 2: Ss in next 2tr and into next 5ch sp, 3ch *(counts as 1tr)*, [2tr, 5ch, 3tr] into same sp, * 3ch, [3tr, 5ch, 3tr] into next 5ch sp; rep from * twice, 3ch, join with ss into 3rd of 3ch.

ROUND 3: 3ch *(counts as 1tr)*, 1tr into each of next 2tr, * [3tr, 5ch, 3tr] into next 5ch sp, 1tr into each of next 3tr, 3ch, 1dc into next 3ch sp, 3ch, ** 1tr into each of next 3tr; rep from * twice and from * to ** once again, join with ss into 3rd of 3ch.

ROUND 4: Ss in each of next 3tr, 3ch *(counts as 1tr)*, 1tr into each of next 2tr, * [3tr, 5ch, 3tr] into next 5ch sp, 1tr into each of next 3tr, 3ch, [1dc into next 3ch sp, 3ch] twice, ** miss next 3tr, 1tr into each of next 3tr; rep from * twice and from * to **

once again, join with ss into 3rd of 3ch.

ROUND 5: 3ch *(counts as 1tr)*, 1tr into each of next 2tr, 2ch, miss 3tr, * [3tr, 5ch, 3tr] into next 5ch sp, 2ch, miss next 3tr, 1tr into each of next 3tr, [2tr into next 3ch sp, 1ch] twice, 2tr into next 3ch sp, ** 1tr into each of next 3tr, 2ch; rep from * twice and from * to ** once again, join with ss into 3rd of 3ch.

ROUND 6: 1ch, 1dc into each tr and ch of previous round, working 3dc into 3rd of 5ch at each corner, join with ss into first dc.

Fasten off yarn.

MIX-AND-MATCH

 125 129 174

99 Baby Bow

11 ≣ Ⓐ

Special abbreviation

MB = make bobble (work 4 open tr in same st leaving 5 loops on hook, draw yarn through all 5 loops at once)

FOUNDATION CHAIN: Work 28ch.

FOUNDATION ROW: *(wrong side)* Work 1dc into 2nd ch from hook, 1dc into each ch to end, turn. *(27dc)*

ROW 1: 1ch, 1dc into each dc, turn. *(27dc)*

ROWS 2 to 5: Rep row 1.

ROW 6: 1ch, [1dc into each of next 3dc, MB] twice, 1dc into each of next 11dc, [MB, 1dc into each of next 3dc] twice, turn.

ROW 7 and every alt row: Rep row 1.

ROW 8: 1ch, 1dc into each of next 5dc, * MB, 1dc into next dc, MB, * 1dc into each of next 11dc; rep from * to * once, 1dc into each of next 5dc, turn.

ROW 10: 1ch, 1dc into each of next 6dc, * MB, 1dc into next dc, MB, * 1dc into each of next 9dc; rep from * to * once, 1dc into each of next 6dc, turn.

ROW 12: 1ch, 1dc into each of next 7dc, * MB, 1dc into next dc, MB, * 1dc into each of next 7dc; rep from * to * once, 1dc into each of next 7dc, turn.

ROW 14: 1ch, 1dc into each of next 8dc, * MB, 1dc into next dc, MB, * 1dc into each of next 5dc; rep from * to * once, 1dc into each of next 8dc, turn.

ROW 16: 1ch, 1dc into each of next 9dc, * MB, 1dc into next dc, MB, * 1dc into each of next 3dc; rep from * to * once, 1dc into each of next 9dc, turn.

ROW 18: 1ch, 1dc into each of next 6dc, * MB, [1dc into next dc, MB] twice, * 1dc into each of next 2dc, MB, 1dc into each of next 2dc; rep from * to * once, 1dc into each of next 6dc, turn.

ROW 20: 1ch, * 1dc into each of next 4dc, MB, 1dc into next dc, MB, 1dc into each of next 4dc, * MB, [1dc into next dc, MB] twice, * once, turn.

ROW 22: 1ch, 1dc into each of next 3dc, * MB, 1dc into next dc, MB, * 1dc into each of next 7dc, MB, 1dc into each of next 7dc; rep from * to * once, 1dc into each of next 3dc, turn.

ROW 24: 1ch, 1dc into each of next 3dc, * MB, 1dc into next dc, MB, * 1dc into each of next 5dc, MB, 1dc into each of next 3dc, MB, 1dc into each of next 5dc; rep from * to * once, 1dc into each of next 3dc, turn.

ROW 26: 1ch, 1dc into each of next 5dc, * MB, [1dc into next dc, MB] twice, * 1dc into each of next 7dc; rep from * to * once, 1dc into each of next 5dc, turn.

ROWS 27 to 32: Rep row 1.
Fasten off yarn.

MIX-AND-MATCH

100 Pastel Delight

1 📷 Ⓐ Ⓑ Ⓒ

FOUNDATION RING: Using yarn A, work 4ch and join with ss to form a ring.

ROUND 1: 3ch *(counts as 1tr)*, 2tr into ring, 2ch, [3tr into ring, 2ch] 3 times, join with ss into 3rd of 3ch. Break off yarn A.

ROUND 2: Join yarn B to any 2ch sp, 3ch *(counts as 1tr)*, [2tr, 2ch, 3tr] into same sp, [3tr, 2ch, 3tr into next 2ch sp] 3 times, join with ss into 3rd of 3ch.

ROUND 3: Ss in each of next 2tr and into next 2ch sp, 3ch *(counts as 1tr)*, [2tr, 2ch, 3tr] into same sp, * 1ch, miss next 2tr, 1tr into each of next 2tr, 1ch, miss next 2tr, ** [3tr, 2ch, 3tr] into next 2ch sp; rep from * twice and from * to ** once again, join with ss into 3rd of 3ch.

ROUND 4: Ss in each of next 2tr and into next 2ch sp, 3ch *(counts as 1tr)*, [2tr, 2ch, 3tr] into same sp, * 1ch, miss next 2tr, 1tr into next tr, 1tr into next ch, 1tr into each of next 2tr, 1tr into next ch, 1tr into next tr, 1ch, miss next 2tr, ** [3tr, 2ch, 3tr] into next 2ch sp; rep from * twice and from * to ** once again, join with ss into 3rd of 3ch. Break off yarn B.

ROUND 5: Join yarn C to any 2ch corner sp, 3ch *(counts as 1tr)*, [2tr, 2ch, 3tr] into same sp, * 1ch, miss 2tr, 1tr into next tr, 1ch, 1tr into each of next 6tr, 1ch, 1tr into next tr, 1ch, miss 2tr, ** [3tr, 2ch, 3tr] into next 2ch corner sp; rep from * twice and from * to ** once again, join with ss into 3rd of 3ch.

ROUND 6: Sl st in each of next 2tr and into next 2ch sp, 3ch *(counts as 1tr)*, [2tr, 3ch, 3tr] into same sp, * 1ch, miss next 2tr, 1tr into next tr, [1ch, 1tr into next tr] twice, 1ch, miss 1tr, 1tr into each of next 2tr, 1ch, miss 1tr, 1tr in next tr [1ch, 1tr in next tr] twice, 1ch, miss 2tr, ** [3tr, 3ch, 3tr] into next 3ch sp; rep from * twice and from * to ** once again, join with ss into 3rd of 3ch.

ROUND 7: Join yarn B to any 3ch corner sp, 3ch *(counts as 1tr)*, [2tr, 3ch, 3tr] into same sp, * 1tr into each of next 3tr, [1ch, 1tr into next tr] 4 times, [1tr into next tr, 1ch] 4 times, 1tr into each of next 3tr, ** [3tr, 3ch, 3tr] into next 3ch corner sp; rep from * twice and from * to ** once again, join with ss into 3rd of 3ch.

ROUND 8: 1ch, 1dc into same place, 1dc into each tr and 1ch sp of previous round, working 3dc into each 3ch corner sp, join with ss into first dc.
Fasten off yarn.

MIX-AND-MATCH

101

Into the Blue

1

A **B** **C** **D**

MIX-AND-MATCH

 116 138 186

FOUNDATION RING: Using yarn A, work 5ch and join with ss to form a ring.

ROUND 1: 3ch *(counts as 1tr)*, 15tr into ring, join with ss into 3rd of 3ch. *(16tr)* Break off yarn A.

ROUND 2: Join yarn B to any st. 3ch *(counts as 1tr)*, 4tr into base of 3ch, * 1tr into each of next 3tr, 5tr into next tr; rep from * to last 3 sts, 1tr into each of next 3tr, join with ss to 3rd of 3ch. *(four corners made)* Break off yarn B.

ROUND 3: Join yarn C to centre st of corner group. 3ch *(counts as 1tr)*, 4tr into base of 3ch, * 1tr into each of next 7tr, 5tr into next tr; rep from * to last 7 sts, 1tr into each of next 7tr, join with ss to 3rd of 3ch. Break off yarn C.

ROUND 4: Join yarn A to centre st of corner group. 3ch *(counts as 1tr)*, [1tr, 2ch 2tr] into base of 3ch, * 1tr into each of next 11tr, [2tr, 2ch, 2tr] into next tr; rep from * to last 11 sts, 1tr into each of next 11tr, join with ss to 3rd of 3ch. Break off yarn C.

ROUND 5: Join yarn D to 2ch sp at corner. 3ch *(counts as 1tr)*, [1tr, 2ch 2tr] into 2ch sp, * 1tr into each of next 15tr, [2tr, 2ch, 2tr] into next tr; rep from * to last 15 sts, 1tr into each of next 15tr, join with ss to 3rd of 3ch. Break off yarn D.

ROUND 6: Join yarn A to 2ch sp at corner. 3ch *(counts as 1tr)*, [1tr, 4ch 2tr] into 2ch sp, * 1tr into each of next 19tr, [2tr, 4ch, 2tr] into next tr; rep from * to last 19 sts, 1tr into each of next 19tr, join with ss to 3rd of 3ch.

ROUND 7: 1ch, 1dc into each tr in previous round, working [2dc, 1ch, 2dc] into each 4ch corner sp, join with ss into first dc.

Fasten off yarn.

102 COLOUR SCHEME Brown, oatmeal and other colours derived from nature are perennial favourites for home furnishings.

103 COLOUR SCHEME: Changing the yarn colours to bright pastel shades surrounded by cream makes the perfect block to combine for a baby afghan.

104 COLOUR SCHEME: Two stripes worked in shades of dark blue show up well against the main turquoise yarn and add an extra zing to the pattern.

OTHER COLOUR SCHEMES

102 **A** **B** **C** **D**

103 **A** **B** **C** **D**

104 **A** **B** **C** **D**

OTHER COLOUR SCHEMES

106 **A** **B** **C** **D**

107 **A** **B** **C** **D**

108 **A** **B** **C** **D**

FOUNDATION CHAIN: Using yarn A, work 29ch.

ROW 1: *(wrong side)* Work 1dc into 2nd ch from hook, work 1dc into each chain along row, turn. *(28dc)*

ROW 2: 1ch, work 1dc into each st along row, turn.

Rep row 2 7 times. Break off yarn A.

Join yarn B and rep row 2 twice. Break off yarn B.

Join yarn C and rep row 2 twice. Break off yarn C.

Join yarn D and rep row 2 21 times. Break off yarn D.

Fasten off yarn.

106 COLOUR SCHEME: Soft, neutral shades combine well in this block which would look good displayed against pine or other light wood furniture.

107 COLOUR SCHEME: Change the colour balance of the original block by using a dark colour to work the lower section of the block.

108 COLOUR SCHEME: Pastel shades of pink, mauve and blue show up well against the deep band of cream at the top of the block.

105

Double Stripes

1 ☰

A **B** **C** **D**

MIX-AND-MATCH

 23 **142** **210**

109

OTHER COLOUR SCHEMES

110

111

112

Four Square

1

MIX-AND-MATCH

 34 **123** **139**

FOUNDATION RING: Using yarn A, work 4ch and join with ss to form a ring.

ROUND 1: 1ch, 12dc into ring, join with ss into first dc.

ROUND 2: 1ch, 1dc into first dc, * 3dc into next dc, 1dc into each of next 2dc; rep from * ending last rep with 1dc, join with ss to first dc. *(four corners made)*

ROUND 3: 1ch, 1dc into each of next 2dc, * 3dc into next dc, 1dc into each of next 4dc; rep from * ending last rep with 2dc, join with ss to first dc.

ROUND 4: 1ch, 1dc into each of next 3dc, * 3dc into next dc, 1dc into each of next 6dc; rep from * ending last rep with 3dc, join with ss to first dc.

Cont working rounds in the same way, working 2 more dc along each side of the square.

After 3 more rounds have been worked, break off yarn A. *(12dc along each side)*

Join yarn B and work one round. *(14dc along each side)* Break off yarn B.

Join yarn C and work two rounds. *(18dc along each side)* Break off yarn C.

Join yarn D and work five rounds. *(28dc along each side)*

Fasten off yarn.

110 COLOUR SCHEME: Warm shades of coral and aubergine combine well with cool shades of green and oatmeal with the darkest colour placed at the centre.

111 COLOUR SCHEME: The large area of soft turquoise worked at the start of this block draws the eye immediately towards the centre of the block.

112 COLOUR SCHEME: A single stripe of bright yellow provides a strong contrast to the rather ordinary colour scheme of three shades of blue.

OTHER COLOUR SCHEMES

114

115

116

Special abbreviations

beg cl = beginning cluster made from 2 tr sts, **cl** = cluster made from 3 tr sts

FOUNDATION RING: Using yarn A, work 4ch and join with ss to form a ring.

ROUND 1: 3ch *(counts as 1tr)*, beg cl into ring, 5ch, * cl into ring, 2ch, ** cl into ring, 5ch; rep from * twice and from * to ** once again, join with ss into 3rd of 3ch. Break off yarn A.

ROUND 2: Join yarn B to any 5ch corner sp, 3ch *(counts as 1tr)*, [beg cl, 2ch, cl] into same sp, * 2ch, 3tr into next 2ch sp, 2ch, ** [cl, 2ch, cl] into next 5ch sp; rep from * twice and from * to ** once again, join with ss into 3rd of 3ch.

ROUND 3: Ss into next 2ch corner sp, 3ch *(counts as 1tr)*, [beg cl, 2ch, cl] into same sp, * 2ch, 2tr into next 2ch sp, 1tr into each of next 3tr, 2tr into next 2ch sp, 2ch, ** [cl, 2ch, cl] into next 2ch sp; rep from * twice and from * to ** once again, join with ss into 3rd of 3ch. Break off yarn B.

ROUND 4: Join yarn C into any 2ch corner sp, 3ch *(counts as 1tr)*, [beg cl, 2ch, cl] into same sp, * 2ch, 2tr into next 2ch sp, 1tr into each of next 7tr, 2tr into next 2ch sp, 2ch, ** [cl, 2ch, cl] into next 2ch sp; rep from * twice and from * to ** once again, join with ss into 3rd of 3ch. Break off yarn C.

ROUND 5: Join yarn D into any 2ch corner sp, 3ch *(counts as 1tr)*, [beg cl, 3ch, cl] into same sp, * 2ch, 2tr into next 2ch sp, 1tr into each of next 11tr, 2tr into next 2ch sp, 2ch, ** [cl, 3ch, cl] into next 2ch sp; rep from * twice and from

* to ** once again, join with ss into 3rd of 3ch.

ROUND 6: Ss into next 3ch corner sp, 3ch *(counts as 1tr)*, [beg cl, 3ch, cl] into same sp, * 2ch, 2tr into next 2ch sp, 1tr into each of next 15tr, 2tr into next 2ch sp, 2ch, ** [cl, 3ch, cl] into next 3ch sp; rep from * twice and from * to ** once again, join with ss into 3rd of 3ch.

ROUND 7: 1ch, 1dc into same place, work 1dc into each tr and the top of each cl of previous round, working 2dc into each 2ch sp and [2dc, 1ch, 2dc] into each 3ch corner sp, join with ss into first dc.

Fasten off yarn.

114 COLOUR SCHEME: This block features an unusual colourway, combining coral and aubergine with vibrant lime green and pale oatmeal.

113

Wisteria

11

MIX-AND-MATCH

 37 **40** **88**

115 COLOUR SCHEME: Purples and a dusky pink work well together in this block while the single stripe of soft, cool green adds contrast.

116 COLOUR SCHEME: The pale blue flower motif draws the eye inwards towards the centre of this strongly patterned block.

117

Granny in the Middle

1 📷

Ⓐ Ⓑ Ⓒ Ⓓ Ⓔ

MIX-AND-MATCH

FOUNDATION RING: Using yarn A, work 6ch and join with ss to form a ring.

ROUND 1: 3ch *(counts as 1tr)*, 2tr into ring, 3ch, * 3tr into ring, 3ch; rep from * twice more, join with ss into 3rd of 3ch. Break off yarn A.

ROUND 2: Join yarn B to any 3ch sp, 3ch, [2tr, 3ch, 3tr] into same sp to make corner, * 1ch, [3tr, 3ch, 3tr] into next 3ch sp to make corner; rep from * twice more, 1ch, join with ss into 3rd of 3ch. Break off yarn B.

ROUND 3: Join yarn C to any 3ch corner sp, 3ch, [2tr, 3ch, 3tr] into same sp, * 1ch, 3tr into ch sp, 1ch, [3tr, 3ch, 3tr] into corner sp; rep from * to end, ending with 1ch, join with ss into 3rd of 3ch. Break off yarn C.

ROUND 4: Join yarn D to any 3ch corner sp, 3ch, [2tr ,3ch, 3tr] into same sp, * [1ch, 3tr into each ch sp] along side of square, 1ch, [3tr, 3ch, 3tr] into corner sp; rep from * to end, ending with 1ch, join with ss into 3rd of 3ch.

Break off yarn D.

ROUND 5: Join yarn E to any 3ch corner sp, 3ch, [2tr, 3ch, 3tr] into same sp, * [1ch, 3tr into each ch sp] along side of square, 1ch, [3tr, 3ch, 3tr] into corner sp; rep from * to end, ending with 1ch, ss into 3rd of 3ch.

ROUND 6: 1ch, work 1dc into each tr of previous round, working 5dc into each 3ch corner sp and 1dc into each 1ch sp, join with ss into first dc.

ROUND 7: 1ch, 1dc into each dc of previous round, working 3dc into centre st of each 5dc corner group, join with ss into first dc. Break off yarn E.

ROUND 8: Join yarn D, 1ch, 1dc into each dc of previous round, working 3dc into centre st of each 3dc corner group, join with ss into first dc. Break off yarn D.

ROUND 9: Join yarn C and rep round 8. Fasten off yarn

118 COLOUR SCHEME: Cool colours such as turquoise and lavender combine with a cool blue-toned grey and the result is very easy on the eye.

119 COLOUR SCHEME: This variation on the classic granny uses a palette of colours graduating outwards from pale pink to dark purple.

120 COLOUR SCHEME: Unlike those used in the blocks 118 and 119, these colours are of a similar mid-tone, giving a different effect to the pattern.

OTHER COLOUR SCHEMES

118 Ⓐ Ⓑ Ⓒ Ⓓ Ⓔ

119 Ⓐ Ⓑ Ⓒ Ⓓ Ⓔ

120 Ⓐ Ⓑ Ⓒ Ⓓ Ⓔ

OTHER COLOUR SCHEMES

122 Ⓐ Ⓑ Ⓒ Ⓓ

123 Ⓐ Ⓑ Ⓒ Ⓓ

124 Ⓐ Ⓑ Ⓒ Ⓓ

FOUNDATION ROW: Using yarn A, work 6ch.

ROW 1: Insert hook into 4th ch from hook, work 3tr, turn.

ROW 2: 3ch *(counts as 1tr)*, 1tr into each of next 2tr, 4tr into loop made by turning ch of previous row, turn.

ROW 3: 3ch *(counts as 1tr)*, 1tr into each of next 2tr, [2tr, 2ch, 2tr] into next tr, 1tr into each of next 2tr, 1tr into 3rd of 3 ch, turn.

ROW 4: 3ch *(counts as 1tr)*, 1 tr into each of next 4tr, [2tr, 2ch, 2tr] into 2ch sp, 1tr into each of next 4tr, 1tr into 3rd of 3ch, turn. Break off yarn A.

ROW 5: Join yarn B, 3ch *(counts as 1tr)*, 1 tr into each of next 6tr, [2tr, 2ch, 2tr] into 2ch sp, 1tr into each of next 6tr, 1tr into 3rd of 3ch, turn. Break off yarn B.

ROW 6: Join yarn A, 3ch *(counts as 1tr)*, 1 tr into each of next 8tr, [2tr, 2ch, 2tr] into 2ch sp, 1tr into each of next 8tr, 1tr into 3rd of 3ch, turn.

ROW 7: 3ch *(counts as 1tr)*, 1 tr into each of next 10tr, [2tr, 2ch, 2tr] into 2ch sp, 1tr into each of next 10tr, 1tr into 3rd of 3ch, turn. Break off yarn A.

ROW 8: Join yarn C, 3ch *(counts as 1tr)*, 1 tr into each of next 12tr, [2tr, 2ch, 2tr] into 2ch sp, 1tr into each of next 12tr, 1tr into 3rd of 3ch, turn. Break off yarn C.

ROW 9: Join yarn A, 3ch *(counts as 1tr)*, 1 tr into each of next 14tr, [2tr, 2ch, 2tr] into 2ch sp, 1tr into each of next 14tr, 1tr into 3rd of 3ch, turn.

ROW 10: 3ch *(counts as 1tr)*, 1 tr into each of next 16tr, [2tr, 2ch, 2tr] into 2ch sp, 1tr into each of next 16tr, 1tr into 3rd of 3ch, turn. Break off yarn A.

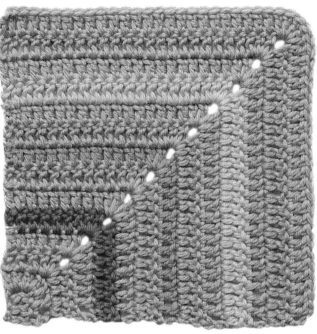

121

ROW 11: Join yarn D, 3ch *(counts as 1tr)*, 1 tr into each of next 18tr, [2tr, 2ch, 2tr] into 2ch sp, 1tr into each of next 18tr, 1tr into 3rd of 3ch. Break off yarn D.

ROW 12: Join yarn A, 3ch *(counts as 1tr)*, 1 tr into each of next 20tr, [2tr, 2ch, 2tr] into 2ch sp, 1tr into each of next 20tr, 1tr into 3rd of 3ch, turn.

ROW 13: 3ch *(counts as 1tr)*, 1 tr into each of next 22tr, [2tr, 2ch, 2tr] into 2ch sp, 1tr into each of next 22tr, 1tr into 3rd of 3ch, turn.

ROW 14: 3ch *(counts as 1tr)*, 1tr into each of next 24tr, 5tr into 2ch sp, 1tr into each of next 24tr, 1tr into 3rd of 3ch. Fasten off yarn.

Coral Seas

1 ☱
Ⓐ Ⓑ Ⓒ Ⓓ

MIX-AND-MATCH

 9
 11
 89

123 **COLOUR SCHEME:** A single stripe worked in bright pink close to one corner adds a note of crisp contrast to the subtle, rather sombre shades used in this scheme.

124 **COLOUR SCHEME:** Changing the position of the strongly coloured stripe changes the emphasis of the striped pattern.

122 **COLOUR SCHEME:** Most neutral shades, including pale greys and beige, look best when combined with a selection of stronger, brighter colours.

125

Triple Stripes

1

Ⓐ Ⓑ Ⓒ Ⓓ

MIX-AND-MATCH

119 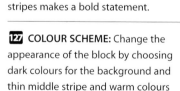148 197

FOUNDATION CHAIN: Using yarn A, work 29ch.

ROW 1: *(wrong side)* Work 1dc into 2nd ch from hook, work 1dc into each chain along row, turn. *(28dc)*

ROW 2: 1ch, work 1dc into each st along row, turn.

Rep row 2 15 times. Break off yarn A.

Join yarn B and rep row 2 four times. Break off yarn B.

Join yarn C and rep row 2 twice. Break off yarn C.

Join yarn D and rep row 2 four times. Break off yarn D.

Join yarn A and rep row 2 seven times. Fasten off yarn.

126 COLOUR SCHEME: This colour scheme combined with the crisp pattern of contrasting horizontal stripes makes a bold statement.

127 COLOUR SCHEME: Change the appearance of the block by choosing dark colours for the background and thin middle stripe and warm colours for the wider stripes.

128 COLOUR SCHEME: Soft, pretty and very feminine, this colour combination would also look good used to make an unusual baby afghan.

OTHER COLOUR SCHEMES

126 Ⓐ Ⓑ Ⓒ Ⓓ

127 Ⓐ Ⓑ Ⓒ Ⓓ

128 Ⓐ Ⓑ Ⓒ Ⓓ

OTHER COLOUR SCHEMES

130

131

132

FOUNDATION RING: Using yarn A, work 4ch and join with ss to form a ring.

ROUND 1: 3ch *(counts as 1tr)*, 3tr into ring, 1ch, * 4tr into ring, 1ch; rep from * twice, join with ss into 3rd of 3ch. Break off yarn A.

ROUND 2: Join yarn B to any 1ch sp, 3ch *(counts as 1tr)*, [3tr, 1ch, 4tr] into next 1ch sp *(corner made)*, 1ch, * [4tr, 1ch, 4tr] into next 1ch sp, 1ch; rep from * twice, join with ss into 3rd of 3ch. *(four corners made)* Break off yarn B.

ROUND 3: Join yarn C, 1ch, 1dc into same place, 1dc into each tr and 1ch sp of previous round, join with ss into first dc. Break off yarn C.

ROUND 4: Join yarn D into any corner dc, 3ch *(counts as 1tr)*, [3tr, 1ch, 4tr] into same dc, 1ch, * miss 4dc, [2tr, 1ch, 2tr] into next dc, 1ch, miss 4dc, ** [4tr, 1ch, 4tr] into next dc, 1ch; rep from * twice and from * to ** once again, join with ss into 3rd of 3ch. Break off yarn D.

ROUND 5: Join yarn E to first tr of any corner group, 3ch *(counts as 1tr)*, work 1tr into each tr of previous round, working 1tr into each 1ch sp along sides of square and [2tr, 1ch, 2tr] into each 1ch corner sp, join with ss into 3rd of 3ch.

ROUNDS 6 & 7: 3ch *(counts as 1tr)*, work 1tr into each tr of previous round, working [2tr, 1ch, 2tr] into each 1ch corner sp, join with ss into 3rd of 3ch. Fasten off yarn.

129

Anemone

1

130 COLOUR SCHEME: The dark background colour makes the bright tones of the flower motif stand out and show off the pattern of the block.

131 COLOUR SCHEME: The rather masculine colours of this block would be perfect for the study, set against leather or tweed upholstery.

132 COLOUR SCHEME: An afghan worked in corals and soft green would look pretty thrown over a rocking chair in a Victorian-style bedroom.

MIX-AND-MATCH

 103 **111** **185**

Sunshine Stripes

MIX-AND-MATCH

19

49

52

Special abbreviation

dc3tog = decrease 2 sts by working the next 3 dc together

FOUNDATION CHAIN: Using yarn A, work 58ch.

FOUNDATION ROW: *(wrong side)* 1dc into 2nd ch from hook, 1dc into each ch, turn. *(57dc)*

ROW 1: 1ch, 1dc into each of next 27dc, dc3tog, 1dc into each of rem 27dc, turn. *(55dc)*

ROW 2: 1ch, 1dc into each of next 26dc, dc3tog, 1dc into each of rem 26dc, turn. *(53dc)*

ROW 3: 1ch, 1dc into each of next 25dc, dc3tog, 1dc into each of rem 25dc, turn. *(51dc)*

ROW 4: 1ch, 1dc into each of next 24dc, dc3tog, 1dc into each of rem 24dc, turn. *(49dc)* Break off yarn A.

Join yarn B. Cont in pattern as set, working dc3tog over 3 centre sts on every row. At the same time, change yarn colours in the following colour sequence:

Work 2 rows in yarn B, 4 rows in yarn A, 2 rows in yarn B.

Join yarn A and cont in pattern until 3dc rem.

NEXT ROW: Work dc3tog.

Fasten off yarn.

OTHER COLOUR SCHEMES

134

135

136

134 COLOUR SCHEME: Mid and light blue are a good colour combination for a baby boy's afghan. For a girl, substitute with shades of pink.

135 COLOUR SCHEME: Changing the colours, so simple mid grey stripes contrast with a plain cream background, gives this block an almost minimalist style.

136 COLOUR SCHEME: Art Deco colours of hot orange and creamy yellow work well on this block decorated with twin L-shaped stripes.

OTHER COLOUR SCHEMES

138 Ⓐ Ⓑ Ⓒ Ⓓ

139 Ⓐ Ⓑ Ⓒ Ⓓ

140 Ⓐ Ⓑ Ⓒ Ⓓ

FOUNDATION RING: Using yarn A, work 6ch and join with ss to form a ring.

ROUND 1: 3ch *(counts as 1tr)*, 3tr into ring, 3ch, [4tr into ring, 3ch] 3 times, join with ss into 3rd of 3ch.

ROUND 2: 5ch *(counts as 1tr, 2ch)*, * miss next 2tr, 1tr into next tr, [2tr, 3ch, 2tr] into next 3ch sp, ** 1tr into next tr, 2ch; rep from * twice and from * to ** once again, join with ss into 3rd of 5ch. Break off yarn A.

ROUND 3: Join yarn B to tr before 2ch sp, 5ch *(counts as 1tr, 2ch)*, * 1tr into each of next 3tr, [2tr, 3ch, 2tr] into next 3ch sp, ** 1tr into each of next 3tr, 2ch; rep from * twice and from * to ** once again, 1tr into each of next 2tr, join with ss into 3rd of 5ch.

ROUND 4: 5ch *(counts as 1tr, 2ch)*, * 1tr into each of next 5tr, [2tr, 3ch, 2tr] into next 3ch sp, ** 1tr into each of next 5tr, 2ch; rep from * twice and from * to ** once again, 1tr into each of next 4tr, join with ss into 3rd of 5ch. Break off yarn B.

ROUND 5: Join yarn C to tr before 2ch sp, 5ch *(counts as 1tr, 2ch)*, * 1tr into each of next 7tr, [2tr, 3ch, 2tr] into next 3ch sp, ** 1tr into each of next 7tr, 2ch; rep from * twice and from * to ** once again, 1tr into each of next 6tr, join with ss into 3rd of 5ch. Break off yarn C.

ROUND 6: Join yarn D to tr before 2ch sp, 5ch *(counts as 1tr, 2ch)*, * 1tr into each of next 9tr, [2tr, 3ch, 2tr] into next 3ch sp, ** 1tr into each of next 9tr, 2ch; rep from * twice and from * to ** once again, 1tr into each of next 8tr, join with ss into 3rd of 5ch.

137

ROUND 7: 1ch, 1dc into same place, work 1dc into each tr of previous round, working 2dc into each 2ch sp and [2dc, 2ch, 2dc] into each 3ch corner sp.

Fasten off yarn.

138 **COLOUR SCHEME:** This colour scheme uses cool shades of blue, turquoise and purple to make a calm and restful visual statement.

139 **COLOUR SCHEME:** Cream, oatmeal and grey are a classic colour combination which enhances the simple striped pattern of this easy-to-crochet block.

140 **COLOUR SCHEME:** Warm shades of yellow, orange and fuchsia pink framed with dark red combine well to make a bright, modern block.

Criss Cross

1
Ⓐ Ⓑ Ⓒ Ⓓ

MIX-AND-MATCH

 46 **63** **203**

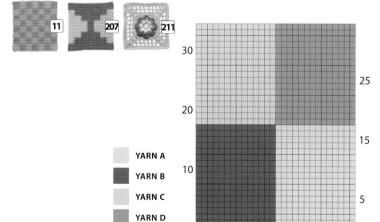

141

Quartet

11 ☰
Ⓐ Ⓑ Ⓒ Ⓓ

MIX-AND-MATCH

11 **207** **211**

FOUNDATION CHAIN: Using yarn A, work 29ch.

WORKING THE PATTERN: When following the chart, read odd-numbered rows (right side rows) from right to left and even-numbered rows (wrong side rows) from left to right.

Starting at the bottom right-hand corner of the chart, work the 34 row pattern from the chart in dc. On the first row, work first dc into 2nd ch from hook, 1dc into each ch along row. *(28dc)*

Fasten off yarn.

142 COLOUR SCHEME: Another symmetrical arrangement of two dark squares set diagonally opposite each other and combined with two paler squares.

143 COLOUR SCHEME: The symmetrical appearance of the block changes here, by simply contrasting one dark square against three squares worked in mid tones.

144 COLOUR SCHEME: Squares worked in variegated yarns look good when set next to squares of matching solid colour. The four squares are arranged symmetrically in this block.

30
25
20
15
10
5

☐ YARN A
■ YARN B
☐ YARN C
■ YARN D

OTHER COLOUR SCHEMES

142

143

144

OTHER COLOUR SCHEMES

146 Ⓐ Ⓑ Ⓒ Ⓓ Ⓔ

147 Ⓐ Ⓑ Ⓒ Ⓓ Ⓔ

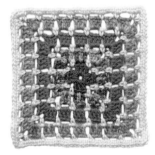

148 Ⓐ Ⓑ Ⓒ Ⓓ Ⓔ

FOUNDATION RING: Using yarn A, work 4ch and join with ss to form a ring.

ROUND 1: 3ch *(counts as 1tr)*, 2tr into ring, 2ch, * 3tr into ring, 2ch; rep from * twice, join with ss into 3rd of 3ch. Break off yarn A.

ROUND 2: Join yarn B to any 2ch sp, 1ch, [1dc, 3ch, 1dc] into same sp, 3ch, * [1dc, 3ch, 1dc] into next 2ch sp, 3ch; rep from * twice, join with ss to first dc. *(four corners made)* Break off yarn B.

ROUND 3: Join yarn C to any 3ch corner sp, 3ch *(counts as 1tr)*, [2tr, 3ch, 3tr] into same sp, 1ch, 3tr into next 3 ch sp, 1ch, * [3tr, 3ch, 3tr] into next 3ch corner sp, 1ch, 3tr into next 3ch sp, 1ch; rep from * twice, join with ss into 3rd of 3ch. Break off yarn C.

ROUND 4: Join yarn B to any 3ch corner sp, 1ch, [1dc, 3ch, 1dc] into same sp, 3ch, [1dc into next 1ch sp, 3ch] twice, * [1dc, 3ch, 1dc] into next 3ch corner sp, 3ch, [1dc into next 1ch sp, 3ch] twice; rep from * twice, join with ss into first dc. Break off yarn B.

ROUND 5: Join yarn D to any 3ch corner sp, 3ch *(counts as 1tr)*, [2tr, 3ch, 3tr] into same sp, 1ch, [3tr into next 3 ch sp, 1ch] 3 times, * [3tr, 3ch, 3tr] into next 3ch corner sp, 1ch, [3tr into next 3ch sp, 1ch] 3 times; rep from * twice, join with ss into 3rd of 3ch. Break off yarn D.

ROUND 6: Join yarn B to any 3ch corner sp, 1ch, [1dc, 3ch, 1dc] into same sp, 3ch, [1dc into next 1ch sp, 3ch] 4 times, * [1dc, 3ch, 1dc] into next 3ch corner sp, 3ch, [1dc into next 1ch sp, 3ch] 4 times; rep from * twice, join with ss into first dc. Break off yarn B.

ROUND 7: Join yarn E to any 3ch corner sp, 3ch *(counts as 1tr)*, [2tr, 3ch, 3tr] into same sp, 1ch, [3tr into next 3 ch sp, 1ch] 5 times, * [3tr, 3ch, 3tr] into next 3ch corner sp, 1ch, [3tr into next 3ch

sp, 1ch] 5 times; rep from * twice, join with ss into 3rd of 3ch. Break off yarn E.

ROUND 8: Join yarn B to any 3ch corner sp, 1ch, [1dc, 3ch, 1dc] into same sp, 3ch, [1dc into next 1ch sp, 3ch] 6 times, * [1dc, 3ch, 1dc] into next 3ch corner sp, 3ch, [1dc into next 1ch sp, 3ch] 6 times; rep from * twice, join with ss into first dc.

ROUND 9: 1ch, 1dc in same place, work 1dc into each dc of previous round and 3dc into each 3ch sp along sides of square, working 5dc into each 3ch corner sp, join with ss into first dc. Fasten off yarn

145

Chocolate Box

1

Ⓐ Ⓑ Ⓒ Ⓓ Ⓔ

MIX-AND-MATCH

 58   **92**   **192**

146 **COLOUR SCHEME:** An unusual colour scheme of blues, greens and pale turquoise shows the block's pattern off to great effect.

147 **COLOUR SCHEME:** Strong, jewel tones zing when surrounded with the very dark berry colour used as the main contrast.

148 **COLOUR SCHEME:** The main contrast has been changed completely from a very dark colour to pale cream.

Solid Square

1

A **B** **C**

MIX-AND-MATCH

 13 **73** **185**

FOUNDATION RING: Using yarn A, work 4ch and join with ss to form a ring.

ROUND 1: 3ch *(counts as 1tr)*, 11tr into ring, join with ss into 3rd of 3ch. *(12tr)*

ROUND 2: 3ch *(counts as 1tr)*, * [2tr, 1dtr] into next tr, [1dtr, 2tr] into next tr, ** 1tr into next tr; rep from * twice and from * to ** once again, join with ss into 3rd of 3ch. Break off yarn A.

ROUND 3: Join yarn B, 3ch *(counts as 1tr)*, 1tr into each of next 2tr, * [2tr, 1dtr] into next dtr, [1dtr, 2tr] into next dtr, ** 1tr into each of next 5tr; rep from * twice and from * to ** once again, 1tr into each of next 2tr, join with ss into 3rd of 3ch. Break off yarn B.

ROUND 4: Join yarn C, 3ch *(counts as 1tr)*, 1tr into each of next 4tr, * [2tr, 1dtr] into next dtr, [1dtr, 2tr] into next dtr, ** 1tr into each of next 9tr; rep from * twice and from * to ** once again, 1tr into each of next 4tr, join with ss into 3rd of 3ch. Break off yarn C.

ROUND 5: Join yarn B, 3ch *(counts as 1tr)*, 1tr into each of next 6tr, * [2tr, 1dtr] into next dtr, [1dtr, 2tr] into next dtr, ** 1tr into each of next 13tr; rep from * twice and from * to ** once again, 1tr into each of next 6tr, join with ss into 3rd of 3ch. Break off yarn B.

ROUND 6: Join yarn A, 3ch *(counts as 1tr)*, 1tr into each of next 8tr, * [2tr, 1dtr] into next dtr, [1dtr, 2tr] into next dtr, ** 1tr into each of next 17tr; rep from * twice and from * to ** once again, 1tr into each of next 8tr, join with ss into 3rd of 3ch.

ROUND 7: 1ch, 1dc into same place, 1dc into each tr of previous round, working [2dc, 1htr] into first dtr of each corner group and [1htr, 2dc] into last dtr of each corner group, join with ss into first dc.

Fasten off yarn.

OTHER COLOUR SCHEMES

A **B** **C**

A **B** **C**

A **B** **C**

150 COLOUR SCHEME: Neutral shades of grey and camel are always a popular colour choice but look even better when combined with a light colour such as cream or white.

151 COLOUR SCHEME: Bright, clashing colours make a strong statement in this block, with the striped pattern showing off the colour arrangement.

152 COLOUR SCHEME: Strong shades of blue and green work well together in this easy-to-make block featuring a strong pattern of stripes.

OTHER COLOUR SCHEMES

154 Ⓐ Ⓑ Ⓒ Ⓓ

155 Ⓐ Ⓑ Ⓒ Ⓓ

156 Ⓐ Ⓑ Ⓒ Ⓓ

Special abbreviation

MB = make bobble (work 4 open tr in same st leaving 5 loops on hook, draw yarn through all 5 loops at once)

FOUNDATION CHAIN: Using yarn A, work 28ch.

FOUNDATION ROW: *(wrong side)* Working first dc into 2nd ch from hook, work 1dc into each ch, turn. *(27dc)*

ROW 1: 1ch, 1dc into each dc, turn.

ROW 2: 1ch, 1dc into each of next 10dc, * MB, 1dc into each of next 2dc; rep from * once, MB, 1dc into each of next 10dc, turn. Break off yarn A.

Join yarn B, rep row 1 three times. Break off yarn B.

Join yarn C, rep row 2, then rep row 1 twice. Break off yarn C.

Join yarn D, rep row 1, then rep row 2, then rep row 1. Break off yarn D.

Join yarn B, rep row 1 twice, then rep row 2. Break off yarn B.

Join yarn C, rep row 1 three times. Break off yarn C.

Join yarn B, rep row 2, then rep row 1 twice. Break off yarn B.

Join yarn D, rep row 1, then rep row 2, then rep row 1. Break off yarn D.

Join yarn C, rep row 1 twice, then rep row 2. Break off yarn C.

Join yarn B, rep row 1 three times. Break off yarn B.

Join yarn A, rep row 2, then rep row 1 twice.

Fasten off yarn.

153

Candy Stripe Bobbles

11 ⌇
Ⓐ Ⓑ Ⓒ Ⓓ

MIX-AND-MATCH

15 **33** **34**

154 COLOUR SCHEME: Another colour scheme based on the neutral palette features in this block where rows of bobbles offer a change of texture at the centre.

155 COLOUR SCHEME: Lots of texture from the regimented rows of bobbles running down the centre of the block contrasts strongly with the bright colours.

156 COLOUR SCHEME: Bright shades of royal blue and jade combine well with softer shades of blue and green to make this lovely colour scheme.

158

Boxed Square

1

MIX-AND-MATCH

170   184   203

FOUNDATION RING: Using yarn A, work 4ch and join with ss to form a ring.

ROUND 1: 1ch, 12dc into ring, join with ss into first dc.

ROUND 2: 1ch, 1dc into first dc, * 3dc into next dc, 1dc into each of next 2dc; rep from * ending last rep with 1dc, join with ss to first dc. *(four corners made)*

ROUND 3: 1ch, 1dc into each of next 2dc, * 3dc into next dc, 1dc into each of next 4dc; rep from * ending last rep with 2dc, join with ss to first dc.

ROUND 4: 1ch, 1dc into each of next 3dc, * 3dc into next dc, 1dc into each of next 6dc; rep from * ending last rep with 3dc, join with ss to first dc.

Cont working rounds in the same way, working 2 more dc along each side of the square.

After 6 more rounds have been worked, break off yarn A. *(18dc along each side)*

Join yarn B and work two rounds. *(22dc along each side)* Break off yarn B.

Join yarn C and work three rounds. *(28dc along each side)*

Fasten off yarn.

158 COLOUR SCHEME: Soft, subtle shades of green combined with pale turquoise make an unusual colour scheme for a baby's room.

159 COLOUR SCHEME: Three shades of the same colour look good when the darkest shade is used to frame the block.

160 COLOUR SCHEME: Change the effect of this block by using the darkest shade at the centre, graduating to the lightest shade round the outside.

159

160

OTHER COLOUR SCHEMES

 162 Ⓐ Ⓑ Ⓒ

 163 Ⓐ Ⓑ Ⓒ

 164 Ⓐ Ⓑ Ⓒ

Special abbreviations

beg cl = beginning cluster made from 2 tr sts, **cl** = cluster made from 3 tr sts

FOUNDATION RING: Using yarn A, work 6ch and join with ss to form a ring.

ROUND 1: 1ch, 12dc into ring, join with ss into first dc.

ROUND 2: 4ch *(counts as 1tr, 1ch)*, * 1tr into next dc, 1ch; rep from * 10 times, join with ss into 3rd of 4ch. *(12 spaced tr)* Break off yarn A.

ROUND 3: Join yarn B to any 1ch sp, 3ch *(counts as 1tr)*, beg cl into same sp, 3ch, * cl into next 1ch sp, 3ch; rep from * 10 times, join with ss into top of beg cl. *(12 clusters)* Break off yarn B.

ROUND 4: Join yarn A to any 3ch sp, 1ch, 4dc into same sp, 4dc into each rem 3ch sp, join with ss into first dc. Break off yarn A.

ROUND 5: Join yarn C into top of any cl, 3ch *(counts as 1tr)*, [1tr, 2ch, 2tr] into same place, * 2ch, miss next 4dc group, 2dc into sp above next cl, 3ch, miss next 4dc group, 2dc into sp above next cl, miss next 4dc group, ** [2tr, 2ch, 2tr] into sp above next cl; rep from * twice and from * to ** once again, join with ss into 3rd of 3ch.

ROUND 6: 3ch *(counts as 1tr)*, 1tr into next tr, * [2tr, 2ch, 2tr] into 2ch corner sp, 1tr into each of next 2tr, 2ch, 1tr into each of next 2dc, 3ch, 1tr into each of next 2dc, 2ch, ** 1tr into each of next 2tr; rep from * twice and from * to ** once again, join with ss into 3rd of 3ch.

ROUND 7: 3ch *(counts as 1tr)*, 1tr into each of next 3tr, * [2tr, 3ch, 2tr] into 2ch

corner sp, 1tr into each of next 4tr, 2ch, 1tr into each of next 2tr, 3ch, 1tr into each of next 2tr, 2ch, ** 1tr into each of next 4tr; rep from * twice and from * to ** once again, join with ss into 3rd of 3ch. Break off yarn C.

ROUND 8: Join yarn A, 3ch *(counts as 1tr)*, work 1tr into each tr and ch of previous round, working 5tr into each 3ch corner sp, join with ss into 3rd of 3ch.

Fasten off yarn.

---

162 **COLOUR SCHEME:** The two lightest colours from block 158 are enhanced by a strong turquoise to make a good choice for the nursery.

---

163 **COLOUR SCHEME:** Two shades of blue combine well with a soft, buttery yellow to show off the intricate centre of this block.

161

Daisy Chain

11 🔄

Ⓐ Ⓑ Ⓒ

MIX-AND-MATCH

 18   31   137

164 **COLOUR SCHEME:** Amethyst and lavender are highlighted with a variegated yarn to make the perfect colour choice for a bed throw in a pretty, feminine bedroom.

Coffee & Cream

11

MIX-AND-MATCH

 47 94 95

FOUNDATION RING: Using yarn A, work 6ch and join with ss to form a ring.

ROUND 1: 3ch *(counts as 1tr)*, 3tr into ring, * 2ch, 4tr into ring; rep from * twice, 2ch, join with ss into 3rd of 3ch.

ROUND 2: Ss in next tr and then between same tr and next tr, 1ch, 1dc into same place, 9tr into next 2ch sp *(corner made)*, * miss next tr, 1dc between next 2tr, 9tr into next 2ch sp; rep from * twice, join with ss into first dc. Break off yarn A.

ROUND 3: Join yarn B to any dc, 3ch *(counts as 1tr)*, 1tr into same place, * 2ch, miss 2tr, 1htr into each of next 2tr, 3tr into next tr, 1htr into each of next 2tr, 2ch, ** miss next 2tr, 2tr into next dc; rep from * twice and from * to ** once again, 2ch, miss 2tr, join with ss into 3rd of 3ch.

ROUND 4: 1ch, 1dc into same place, 1dc into next tr, * 2dc into next 2ch sp, 1dc into each of next 2htr, 1dc into next tr, 4ch, miss 1tr, 1dc into next tr, 1dc into each of next 2htr, 2dc into 2ch sp; ** 1tr into each of next 2tr; rep from * twice and from * to ** once again, join with ss into first dc. Break off yarn B.

ROUND 5: Join yarn C to any 4ch sp, 3ch *(counts as 1tr)*, 8tr into same sp, * miss 2dc, 1dc into next dc, 2ch, miss 2dc, 1dc into each of next 2dc, 2ch, miss 2dc, 1dc into next dc, miss 2dc, ** 9tr into next 4ch sp; rep from * twice and from * to ** once again, join with ss into 3rd of 3ch.

ROUND 6: 1ch, 1dc into same place, 1dc into each of next 3tr, [1htr, 1tr, 1htr] into next tr, 1dc into each of next 4tr, * 1dc into next dc, 2ch, 1dc into each of next 2dc, 2ch, 1dc into next dc, ** 1dc into each of next 4tr, [1htr, 1tr, 1htr] into next tr, 1dc into each of next 4tr; rep from * twice and from * to ** once again, join with ss into first dc.

ROUND 7: 1ch, 1dc into same place, 1dc into each of next 4dc, * 1dc into next htr, 3dc into next tr, 1dc into next htr, 1dc into each of next 5dc, 2ch, 1dc into each of next 2dc, 2ch, ** 1dc into each of next 5dc; rep from * twice and from * to ** once again, 1dc into next dc, join with ss into first dc.

ROUND 8: 3ch *(counts as 1tr)*, 1tr into each of next 5dc, * 5tr into next dc, 1tr into each of next 7dc, 2ch, 1tr into each of next 2tr, 2ch, ** 1tr into each of next 7dc; rep from * twice and from * to ** once again, 1tr into next dc, join with ss into 3rd of 3ch.

ROUND 9: 3ch *(counts as 1tr)*, 1tr into each tr and ch of previous round, working 5tr into centre st of each 5tr corner group, join with ss into 3rd of 3ch.

Fasten off yarn.

OTHER COLOUR SCHEMES

166 A B C

167 A B C

168   A B C

166 **COLOUR SCHEME:** Warm yellows and oranges look good against natural pine and beech furniture.

167 **COLOUR SCHEME:** The dark background enhances the flower motif.

168 **COLOUR SCHEME:** Three bright, strongly contrasting colours show off the block's intricate structure.

165

OTHER COLOUR SCHEMES

170 Ⓐ Ⓑ Ⓒ Ⓓ Ⓔ Ⓕ Ⓖ Ⓗ

171 Ⓐ Ⓑ Ⓒ Ⓓ Ⓔ Ⓕ Ⓖ Ⓗ

172 Ⓐ Ⓑ Ⓒ Ⓓ Ⓔ Ⓕ Ⓖ Ⓗ

FOUNDATION CHAIN: Using yarn A, work 29ch.

WORKING THE PATTERN: When following the chart, read odd-numbered rows (right side rows) from right to left and even-numbered rows (wrong side rows) from left to right. Starting at the bottom right-hand corner of the chart, work the 34 row pattern from the chart in dc. On the first row, work first dc into 2nd ch from hook, 1dc into each ch along row. *(28dc)*

Fasten off yarn.

170 COLOUR SCHEME: Autumn leaf colours are always pleasing to look at—the different shades combine well in this block.

171 COLOUR SCHEME: Solid and variegated shades of one single colour change the appearance of this block and make the stripes blend together and look more harmonious.

172 COLOUR SCHEME: Eight strong, clashing colours makes each stripe stand out against its neighbours. This colour scheme would make a cheerful throw for a child's bedroom.

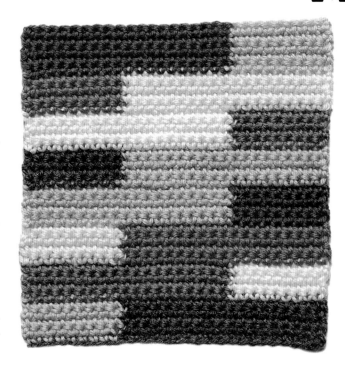

169

Interlocking Stripes

11 ≋
Ⓐ Ⓑ Ⓒ D E Ⓕ Ⓖ Ⓗ

MIX-AND-MATCH

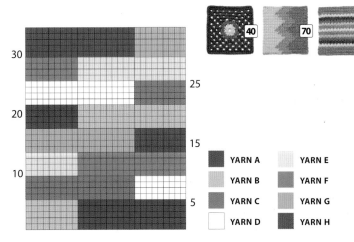

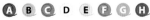

	YARN A		YARN E
	YARN B		YARN F
	YARN C		YARN G
	YARN D		YARN H

173

Big Round

11 📷

Ⓐ Ⓑ

MIX-AND-MATCH

 104 138 199

Special abbreviations

beg cl = beginning cluster made from 3 tr sts, **cl** = cluster made from 4 tr sts

FOUNDATION RING: Using yarn A, work 6ch and join with ss to form a ring.

ROUND 1: 1ch, 12dc into ring, join with ss into first dc.

ROUND 2: 4ch *(counts as 1tr, 1ch)*, * 1tr into next dc, 1ch; rep from * 10 times, join with ss into 3rd of 4ch. *(12 spaced tr)*

ROUND 3: Ss into next 1ch sp, 3ch *(counts as 1tr)*, beg cl into same sp, 3ch, * cl into next 1ch sp, 3ch; rep from * 10 times, join with ss into top of beg cl. *(12 clusters)*

ROUND 4: Ss into next 3ch sp, 3ch *(counts as 1tr)*, beg cl into same sp, * 2ch, 1tr into top of next cl, 2ch, ** cl into next 3ch sp; rep from * 10 times and from * to ** once again, join with ss into top of beg cl.

ROUND 5: 1ch, 3dc into each 2ch sp of previous round, join with ss into first dc. Break off yarn A.

ROUND 6: Join yarn B into top of any cl, 3ch *(counts as 1tr)*, [1tr, 2ch, 2tr] into same place, * [2ch, miss next 3dc group, 1dc into sp between next two 3dc groups] 5 times, 2ch, ** [2tr, 2ch, 2tr] into sp above next cl; rep from *

twice and from * to ** once again, join with ss into 3rd of 3ch.

ROUND 7: 3ch *(counts as 1tr)*, 1tr into next tr, * [2tr, 3ch, 2tr] into 2ch corner sp, 1tr into each of next 2tr, 2ch, 1tr into next dc, [2ch, 1dc into next dc] 3 times, 2ch, 1tr into next dc, 2ch, ** 1tr into each of next 2tr; rep from * twice and from * to ** once again, join with ss into 3rd of 3ch.

ROUND 8: 3ch *(counts as 1tr)*, 1tr into each of next 3tr, * [2tr, 3ch, 2tr] into 2ch corner sp, 1tr into each of next 4tr, 2ch, 1tr into next tr, [2ch, 1tr into next dc] 3 times, 2ch, 1tr into next tr, 2ch, ** 1tr into each of next 4tr; rep from * twice and from * to ** once again, join with ss into 3rd of 3ch.

ROUND 9: 1ch, 1dc into same place, 1dc into each of next 5tr, * 5dc into 3ch corner sp, 1dc into each of next 6tr, [2dc into next 2ch sp] 6 times, ** 1dc into each of next 6tr; rep from * twice and from * to ** once again, join with ss into first dc.

Fasten off yarn.

174 COLOUR SCHEME: This is such a pretty block to use for making a baby girl's afghan. You can the same pattern to make one for a baby boy, but substitute a variegated blue yarn for the centre motif.

175 COLOUR SCHEME: This subtle, rather sophisticated colour scheme of earth tones will look good displayed with natural materials such as natural wood, leather and terracotta.

176 COLOUR SCHEME: By contrasting a pale centre motif against a dark background, the appearance of this block changes drastically.

174   Ⓐ Ⓑ

175   Ⓐ Ⓑ

176   Ⓐ Ⓑ

OTHER COLOUR SCHEMES

178 Ⓐ Ⓑ Ⓒ Ⓓ

179 Ⓐ Ⓑ Ⓒ Ⓓ

180 Ⓐ Ⓑ Ⓒ Ⓓ

FOUNDATION CHAIN: Using yarn A, work 29ch.

WORKING THE PATTERN: When following the chart, read odd-numbered rows (right side rows) from right to left and even-numbered rows (wrong side rows) from left to right.

Starting at the bottom right-hand corner of the chart, work the 34 row pattern from the chart in dc. On the first row, work first dc into 2nd ch from hook, 1dc into each ch along row. *(28dc)*

Fasten off yarn.

178 **COLOUR SCHEME:** Pale shades of pink and cream are used to work the pattern of rectangles so they contrast strongly against the hot pink background.

179 **COLOUR SCHEME:** Change the tonal balance of the original block by using a light colour to work the background and contrasting darker shades for the rectangles.

180 **COLOUR SCHEME:** This really attractive colour scheme contrasts rectangles worked in berry and wine shades set on a lavender-coloured background.

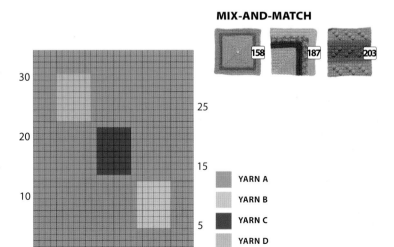

177

Trio

11 ⊜
Ⓐ Ⓑ Ⓒ Ⓓ

MIX-AND-MATCH

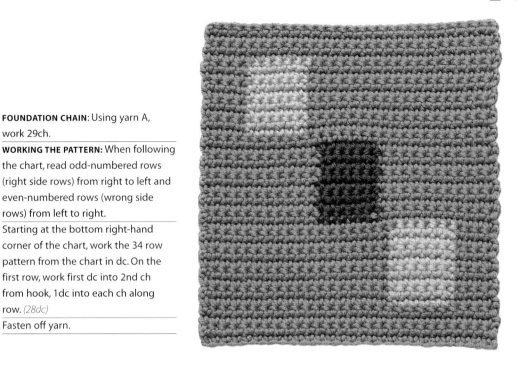

158   187   203

	YARN A	
	YARN B	
	YARN C	
	YARN D	

30
25
20
15
10
5

181

Begonia

11

Ⓐ Ⓑ Ⓒ Ⓓ Ⓔ

MIX-AND-MATCH

14 130 144

Special abbreviations

beg cl = beginning cluster made from 3 dtr sts, **cl** = cluster made from 4 dtr sts

FOUNDATION RING: Using yarn A, work 8ch and join with ss to form a ring.

ROUND 1: 4ch *(counts as 1dtr)*, beg cl, * 4ch, cl; rep from * 6 times, 4ch, join with ss into 4th of 4ch. Break off yarn A.

ROUND 2: Join yarn B to any 4ch sp, 3ch *(counts as 1tr)*, 3tr into same 4ch sp, * 4tr into next 4ch sp, 6ch, ** 4tr into next 4ch sp; rep from * twice and from * to ** once again, join with ss into 3rd of 3ch.

ROUND 3: 3ch *(counts as 1tr)*, 1tr into each of next 7tr, * [3tr, 3ch, 3tr] into next 6ch sp, ** 1tr into each of next 8tr; rep from * twice and from * to ** once again, join with ss into 3rd of 3ch. Break off yarn B.

ROUND 4: Join yarn C to any 3ch sp, 3ch *(counts as 1tr)*, [1tr, 3ch, 2tr] into same 3ch sp, * 1tr into each of next 14tr, ** [2tr, 3ch, 2tr] into next 3ch sp; rep from * twice and from * to ** once again, join with ss into 3rd of 3ch. Break off yarn C.

ROUND 5: Join yarn D to any 3ch sp, 3ch *(counts as 1tr)*, [1tr, 3ch, 2tr] into same 3ch sp, * 1tr into each of next 18tr, ** [2tr, 3ch, 2tr] into next 3ch sp; rep from * twice and from * to ** once again, join with ss into 3rd of 3ch. Break off yarn D.

ROUND 6: Join yarn E, 1ch, 1dc into each tr of previous round, working [2dc, 1ch, 2dc] into each 3ch sp, join with ss into first dc.

ROUND 7: 1ch, 1dc into each dc of previous round, working 3dc into each 1ch corner sp, join with ss into first dc. Fasten off yarn.

182 COLOUR SCHEME: A light colour such as cream used to crochet the first part of a block worked in rounds will take your eye straight to the centre of the pattern.

183 COLOUR SCHEME: Bright yellow adds interest to this colourway worked mainly in shades of dark-toned blues and light-toned turquoises.

184 COLOUR SCHEME: Greens and browns are a very masculine colour scheme, particularly when used for a throw displayed against leather or dark wood furniture.

OTHER COLOUR SCHEMES

182 Ⓐ Ⓑ Ⓒ Ⓓ Ⓔ

183 Ⓐ Ⓑ Ⓒ Ⓓ Ⓔ

184 Ⓐ Ⓑ Ⓒ Ⓓ Ⓔ

185

OTHER COLOUR SCHEMES

186

187

188

Special abbreviation

dc3tog = decrease 2 sts by working the next 3 dc together.

FOUNDATION CHAIN: Using yarn A, work 58ch.

FOUNDATION ROW: *(right side)* 1dc into 2nd ch from hook, 1dc into each ch, turn. *(57dc)*

ROW 1: 1ch, 1dc into each of next 27dc, miss 1dc, 1dc into next dc, miss 1dc, 1dc into each of rem 27dc, turn. *(55dc)*

ROW 2: 1ch, 1dc into each of next 26dc, miss 1dc, 1dc into next dc, miss 1dc, 1dc into each of rem 26dc, turn. *(53dc)*

ROW 3: 1ch, 1dc into each of next 25dc, miss 1dc, 1dc into next dc, miss 1dc, 1dc into each of rem 25dc, turn. *(51dc)*

ROW 4: 1ch, 1dc into each of next 24dc, miss 1dc, 1dc into next dc, miss 1dc, 1dc into each of rem 24dc, turn. *(49dc)*

Break off yarn A.

Join yarn B. Cont in pattern as set, dec 1 st at each side of centre st on every row. At the same time, change yarn colours in the following colour sequence:

Work 4 rows in yarn B, 4 rows in yarn C. Join yarn D and cont in pattern until 3dc rem.

NEXT ROW: Work dc3tog.

Fasten off yarn.

In the Pink

186 **COLOUR SCHEME**: A bright, hot shade of yellow is used to give this block a strongly-defined outside edge as it contrasts well with the other colours which are cool in tone.

187 **COLOUR SCHEME**: This choice of colours would be perfect for making a small, strongly patterned afghan for a baby boy.

188 **COLOUR SCHEME**: The variegated yarn used in this block shades from green to brown through beige and adds interest to the striped pattern.

MIX-AND-MATCH

 35   **77**   **97**

189

Willow

11 📷

OTHER COLOUR SCHEMES

190

191

192

MIX-AND-MATCH

 19 **46** **199**

FOUNDATION RING: Using yarn A, work 6ch and join with ss to form a ring.

ROUND 1: 3ch *(counts as 1tr)*, 15tr into ring, join with ss into 3rd of 3ch. *(16tr)*

ROUND 2: 4ch *(counts as 1tr, 1ch)*, [1tr into next tr, 1ch] 15 times, join with ss into 3rd of 4ch. Break off yarn A.

ROUND 3: Join yarn B to any tr of previous round, 3ch *(counts as 1tr)*, [2tr into next 1ch sp, 1tr into next tr] 15 times, join with ss into 3rd of 3ch. *(48tr)*

ROUND 4: 1ch, 1dc into same place, * 5ch, ss into 5th ch from hook, miss next 2tr, 1dc into next tr, 2ch, miss next 2tr, 1dc into next tr, 3ch, miss next 2tr, 1dc into next tr, 2ch, miss next 2tr, ** 1dc into next tr; rep from * twice and from * to ** once again, join with ss into first dc.

ROUND 5: Ss into next 5ch sp, 3ch *(counts as 1tr)*, [4tr, 3ch, 5tr] into same sp, *1dc into next 2ch sp, 5tr into next 3ch sp, 1dc into next 2ch sp, ** [5tr, 3ch, 5tr] into next 5ch sp; rep from * twice and from * to ** once more, join with ss into 3rd of 3ch. Break off yarn B.

ROUND 6: Join yarn C to any corner 3ch sp, 1ch, [1dc, 3ch, 1dc] into same place, * 5ch, 1tr into next dc, 3ch, miss next 2tr, 1dc into next tr, 3ch, miss next 2tr,

1tr into next dc, 5ch, ** [1dc, 3ch, 1dc] into next 3ch sp; rep from * twice and from * to ** once again, join with ss into first dc.

ROUND 7: Ss into next 3ch sp, 3ch *(counts as 1tr)*, [2tr, 2ch, 3tr] into same 3ch sp, * 5tr into next 5ch sp, 3tr into each of next 2 3ch sps, 5tr into next 5ch sp, ** [3tr, 2ch, 3tr] into next 3ch sp; rep from * twice and from * to ** once again, join with ss into 3rd of 3ch. Break off yarn C.

ROUND 8: Join yarn A, 1ch, 1dc into each tr of previous round, working [2dc, 2ch, 2dc] into each 2ch corner sp, join with ss into first dc.

ROUND 9: 1ch, 1dc into each dc of previous round, working 3dc into each 2ch corner sp, join with ss into first dc. Fasten off yarn.

190 **COLOUR SCHEME:** A soft, warm amber shade combines well with bright shades of yellow and orange to work this intricately patterned block.

191 **COLOUR SCHEME:** The centre motif graduates outwards from a light centre to dark outside band, then the lightest colour is used to frame the block.

192 **COLOUR SCHEME:** To give a different effect from the previous block, the three colours used here graduate outwards from dark to light, then the dark colour is repeated round the edge.

OTHER COLOUR SCHEMES

194 Ⓐ Ⓑ Ⓒ Ⓓ Ⓔ

195 Ⓐ Ⓑ Ⓒ Ⓓ Ⓔ

196 Ⓐ Ⓑ Ⓒ Ⓓ Ⓔ

FOUNDATION CHAIN: Using yarn A, work 32ch, turn.

FOUNDATION ROW: *(right side)* 2dc into 4th ch from hook, * miss 1ch, 2dc into next ch; rep from * to end, turn. *(30dc)*

ROW 1: 2ch, * miss 1dc, 2dc into next dc; rep from * to end, turn.

Rep row 1 four times. Break off yarn A.

Join yarn B and rep row 1 twice. Break off yarn B.

Join yarn C and rep row 1 twice. Break off yarn C.

Join yarn D and rep row 1 twice. Break off yarn D.

Join yarn C and rep row 1 twice. Break off yarn C.

Join yarn E and rep row 1 twice. Break off yarn E.

Join yarn B and rep row 1 twice. Break off yarn B.

Join yarn C and rep row 1 twice. Break off yarn C.

Join yarn A and rep row 1 six times. Break off yarn A.

Join yarn C and rep row 1 eight times. Fasten off yarn.

193

Textured Stripes

1 ⬓

Ⓐ Ⓑ Ⓒ Ⓓ Ⓔ

194 COLOUR SCHEME: A textured surface plus stripes of colour work well in this lively colour scheme of yellow highlighted with soft turquoise.

195 COLOUR SCHEME: Variegated yarns add extra surface interest. Purple and dull pink come to life with the two stripes of bright lime green.

196 COLOUR SCHEME: Capri blue and a deep, vibrant shade of kingfisher blue, looks good combined with stripes worked in pale, ice cream colours.

MIX-AND-MATCH

 4   **18**   **64**

Fretwork

11

MIX-AND-MATCH

 14 35 212

FOUNDATION RING: Using yarn A, work 6ch and join with ss to form a ring.

ROUND 1: 3ch *(counts as 1tr)*, 2tr into ring, 3ch, * 3tr into ring, 3ch; rep from * twice more, join with ss into 3rd of 3ch.
Break off yarn A.

ROUND 2: Join yarn B to any 3ch sp, 3ch, [2tr, 3ch, 3tr] into same sp to make corner, * 1ch, [3tr, 3ch, 3tr] into next 3ch sp to make corner; rep from * twice more, 1ch, join with ss into 3rd of 3ch. Break off yarn B.

ROUND 3: Join yarn C to any 1ch sp, 1ch, 1dc into same sp, 1dc into each tr and 1ch sp of previous round, working 5dc into each 3ch corner sp, join with ss into first dc.

ROUND 4: 4ch *(counts as 1tr, 1ch)*, miss 1dc, [1tr into next dc, 1ch, miss 1dc] twice, * [1tr, 1ch, 1tr, 1ch, 1tr] into next dc to form corner, 1ch, miss 1dc, ** [1tr into next dc, 1ch, miss 1dc] 5 times; rep from * twice and from * to ** once again, [1tr into next dc, 1ch, miss 1dc] twice, join with ss into 3rd of 4ch. Break off yarn C.

ROUND 5: Join yarn D into any tr along one side of square, 1ch, 1dc into same place, 1dc into each tr and 1ch sp of previous round, working 3dc into centre tr of each corner group, join with ss into first dc.

ROUND 6: 4ch *(counts as 1tr, 1ch)*, miss 1dc, [1tr into next dc, 1ch, miss 1dc] 3 times, 1tr into next dc, 1ch, * [1tr, 1ch, 1tr, 1ch, 1tr] into next dc to form corner, 1ch, ** [1tr into next dc, 1ch, miss 1dc] 8 times, 1tr into next dc, 1ch; rep from * twice and from * to ** once again, [1tr into next dc, 1ch, miss 1dc] 4 times, join with ss into 3rd of 4ch.

ROUND 7: 1ch, 1dc into same place, 1dc into each tr and 1ch sp of previous round, working 3dc into centre tr of each corner group, join with ss into first dc. Break off yarn D.

ROUND 8: Join yarn B into any dc along one side of square, 1ch, 1dc into same place, 1dc into each dc of previous round, working 3dc into centre st of each 3dc corner group, join with ss into first dc. Break off yarn B.

ROUND 9: Join yarn A and rep round 8. Break off yarn A.

ROUND 10: Join yarn C, 1ch, 1dc into same place, 1dc into each dc of previous round, working 2dc into centre st of each 3dc corner group, join with ss into first dc.
Fasten off yarn.

 COLOUR SCHEME: Change the colour balance of this block by contrasting salmon and coral shades with a clear, mid-toned blue.

 COLOUR SCHEME: Bright turquoise enlivens a subtle colour combination of three soft greens with a wide band of contrast.

 COLOUR SCHEME: An afghan worked in bright, cheerful colours such as yellow and orange will add life and warmth to any neutral decorating scheme.

OTHER COLOUR SCHEMES

198

199

200

OTHER COLOUR SCHEMES

202

 Ⓐ Ⓑ Ⓒ

203

 Ⓐ Ⓑ Ⓒ

204

 Ⓐ Ⓑ Ⓒ

Special abbreviation

MB = make bobble (work 4 open tr in same st leaving 5 loops on hook, draw yarn through all 5 loops at once)

FOUNDATION CHAIN: Using yarn A, work 28ch.

FOUNDATION ROW: *(wrong side)* Working first dc into 2nd ch from hook, work 1dc into each ch, turn. *(27dc)*

ROW 1: 1ch, 1dc into each dc, turn.

ROW 2: 1ch, 1dc into each of next 7dc, * MB, 1dc into each of next 7dc; rep from *, ending last rep with 1dc into each of next 3dc, turn.

ROWS 3 & 5: Rep row 1.

ROW 4: 1ch, 1dc into each of next 5dc, MB, 1dc into each of next 7dc; rep from *, ending last rep with 1dc into each of next 5dc, turn.

ROW 6: 1ch, 1dc into each of next 3dc, MB, 1dc into each of next 7dc; rep from *, ending last rep with 1dc into each of next 7dc, turn.

ROWS 7 & 8: Rep row 1. Break off yarn A. Join yarn B and rep row 1 three times. Break off yarn B.

ROWS 12 & 13: Join yarn C and rep row 1.

ROW 14: Rep row 6.

ROWS 15 & 17: Rep row 1.

ROW 16: Rep row 4.

ROW 18: Rep row 2.

ROWS 19 & 20: Rep row 1. Break off yarn C.

Join yarn B and rep row 1 three times. Break off yarn B.

Join yarn A and rep row 1 twice, then rep rows 2 to 8.

Fasten off yarn.

201

Zigzag Bobbles

11 ⇌
Ⓐ Ⓑ Ⓒ

202 **COLOUR SCHEME:** Bobbles make an interesting texture, especially when contrasted with smooth stripes of colour in blue and coral.

203 **COLOUR SCHEME:** Green and turquoise look good together, particularly this clear asparagus green and deep, blue-toned turquoise.

203 **COLOUR SCHEME:** This block would be a good choice for making cushions and a small throw for a rocking chair in a sunny breakfast room.

MIX-AND-MATCH

 41 **44** **180**

205

Hourglass

FOUNDATION CHAIN: Using yarn A, work 29ch.

WORKING THE PATTERN: When following the chart, read odd-numbered rows (right side rows) from right to left and even-numbered rows (wrong side rows) from left to right.

Starting at the bottom right-hand corner of the chart, work the 34 row pattern from the chart in dc. On the first row, work first dc into 2nd ch from hook, 1dc into each ch along row. (28dc)

Fasten off yarn.

MIX-AND-MATCH

45 **127** **136**

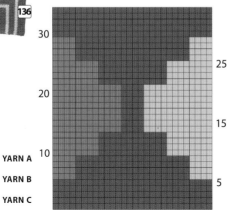

YARN A
YARN B
YARN C

OTHER COLOUR SCHEMES

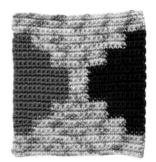

206

207

208

206 **COLOUR SCHEME:** Variegated blue and cream yarn used for the hourglass shape makes a striking contrast to the plain areas of mid and dark shades of blue.

207 **COLOUR SCHEME:** Use a dark colour to accentuate the hourglass shape and set it against two paler contrasts which have a similar tone.

208 **COLOUR SCHEME:** Two strong but harmonious colours show up well against cream, a versatile colour which looks as good with bright colours as with neutral shades.

OTHER COLOUR SCHEMES

210

211 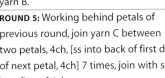 A B C D

212

FOUNDATION RING: Using yarn A, work 6ch and join with ss to form a ring.

ROUND 1: 5ch *(counts as 1tr, 2ch)*, [1tr into ring, 2ch] 7 times, join with ss into 3rd of 5ch.

ROUND 2: Ss into next 2ch sp, 1ch, [1dc, 1htr, 1tr, 1htr, 1dc] into same sp *(petal made)*, [1dc, 1htr, 1tr, 1htr, 1dc] into each rem 2ch sp, join with ss into first dc. Break off yarn A.

ROUND 3: Working behind petals of previous round, join yarn B between two petals, 3ch, [ss into back of first dc of next petal, 3ch] 7 times, join with ss into first of 3ch.

ROUND 4: Ss into next 3ch sp, 1ch, [1dc, 2htr, 1tr, 2htr, 1dc] into same sp, [1dc, 2htr, 1tr, 2htr, 1dc] into each rem 3ch sp, join with ss into first dc. Break off yarn B.

ROUND 5: Working behind petals of previous round, join yarn C between two petals, 4ch, [ss into back of first dc of next petal, 4ch] 7 times, join with ss into first of 4ch.

ROUND 6: Ss into next 4ch sp, 1ch, [1dc, 2htr, 3tr, 2htr, 1dc] into same sp, [1dc, 2htr, 3tr, 2htr, 1dc] into each rem 4ch sp, join with ss into first dc. Break off yarn C.

ROUND 7: Working behind petals of previous round, join yarn D between two petals, 5ch, [ss into back of first dc of next petal, 5ch] 7 times, join with ss into first of 5ch.

ROUND 8: Ss into next 5ch sp, 1ch, 6dc into same sp, * [3tr, 2ch, 3tr] into next 5ch sp *(corner made)*, ** 6dc into next 5ch sp; rep from * twice and from * to ** once again, join with ss into first dc.

ROUND 9: 3ch *(counts as 1tr)*, 1tr into each dc and tr of previous round, working [2tr, 2ch, 2tr] into each 2ch corner sp, join with ss into 3rd of 3ch.

ROUND 10: Ss into next tr, 5ch *(counts as 1tr, 2ch)*, miss 2tr, 1tr into next tr, [2ch, miss 2tr, 1 tr into next tr] twice, * [3tr, 2ch, 3tr] into next 2ch corner sp, ** [1tr into next tr, 2ch, miss 2tr] 5 times, 1tr into next tr; rep from * twice and from * to ** once again, 1tr into next tr, 2ch, miss 2tr, 1tr into next tr, 2ch, join with ss into 3rd of 5ch.

ROUND 11: 5ch *(counts as 1tr, 2ch)*, [1tr into next tr, 2ch] 3 times, miss 2tr, 1tr into next tr, * [3tr, 2ch, 3tr] into next 2ch corner sp, 1tr into next tr, 2ch, miss 2tr, ** [1tr into next tr, 2ch] 6 times, miss 2tr, 1tr into next tr; rep from * twice and from * to ** once again, [1tr into next tr, 2ch] twice, join with ss into 3rd of 5ch.

ROUND 12: 1ch, 1dc into same place, 1dc into each tr of previous round, working 2dc into each 2ch sp along sides of square and 3dc into each 2ch corner sp, join with ss into first dc.

209

Marigold

111

A B C D

MIX-AND-MATCH

 140 **155** **166**

ROUND 13: 1ch, 1dc into same place, 1dc into each dc of previous round, working 3dc into centre st of each 3dc corner group, join with ss into first dc.

Fasten off yarn.

210 **COLOUR SCHEME:** Variety of blues.

211 **COLOUR SCHEME:** Coral and cream.

212 **COLOUR SCHEME:** Amethyst, pinks.

Techniques

In this chapter, you'll find a refresher course to help you make and join the blocks shown in the directory, including tips on joining yarns and working a coloured pattern from a chart. There are also patterns for making a variety of pretty edgings and details of the actual yarns used to work the blocks.

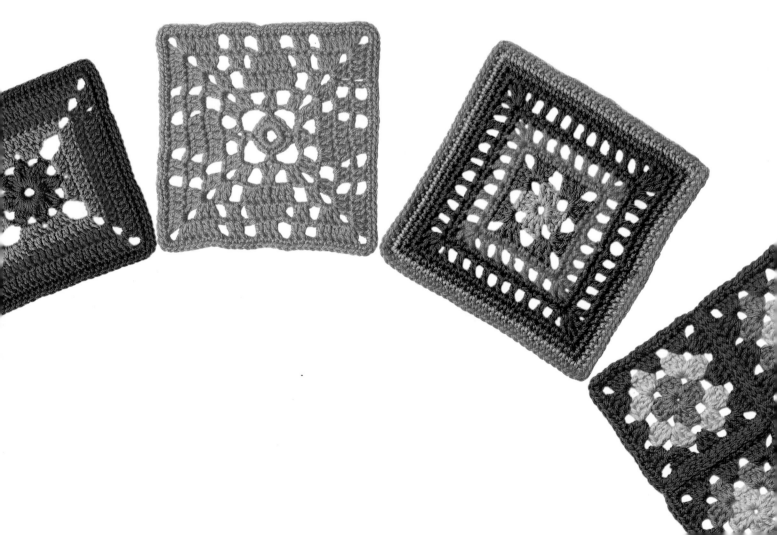

How to start

Holding the hook and yarn

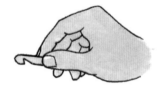

1 Holding the hook as if it was a pen is the most widely used method. Centre the tips of your right thumb and forefinger over the flat section of the hook.

2 An alternative way to hold the hook is to grasp the flat section of the hook between your right thumb and forefinger as if you were holding a knife.

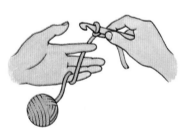

3 To control the supply and keep an even tension on the yarn, loop the short end of the yarn over your left forefinger and take the yarn coming from the ball loosely around the little finger on the same hand. Use the middle finger on the same hand to help hold the work. If left-handed, hold the hook in the left hand and the yarn in the right.

Working a foundation chain (ch)

The foundation chain is the equivalent of casting on in knitting and it's important to make sure that you have made the required number of chains for the pattern you are going to work. Count each V-shaped loop on the front of the chain as one chain stitch, except for the loop on the hook which is not counted. You may find it easier to turn the chain over and count the stitches on the back of the chain. When working the first row of stitches (usually called the foundation row) into the chain, insert the hook under one thread or two, depending on your preference.

1 Holding the hook with the slip knot in your right hand and the yarn in your left, wrap the yarn over the hook. Draw the yarn through to make a new loop and complete the first chain stitch.

2 Repeat this step, drawing a new loop of yarn through the loop already on the hook until the chain is the required length. Move the thumb and forefinger that are grasping the chain upward after every few stitches to keep the tension even. When working into the chain, insert the hook under one thread (for a looser edge) or two (for a firmer edge), depending on your preference.

Making a slip knot

1 Loop the yarn as shown, insert the hook into the loop, catch the yarn with the hook and pull it through to make a loop over the hook.

2 Gently pull the yarn to tighten the loop around the hook and complete the slip knot.

Turning chains

When working crochet in rows or rounds, you will need to work a specific number of extra chains at the beginning of each row or round. The extra chains are needed to bring the hook up to the correct height for the particular stitch you will be working next. When the work is turned at the end of a straight row, the extra chains are called a turning chain, and when they are worked at the beginning of a round, they are called a starting chain.

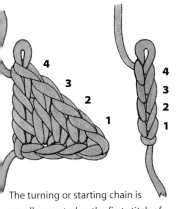

The turning or starting chain is usually counted as the first stitch of the row, except when working double crochet where the single turning chain is ignored. For example, *3ch (counts as 1tr)* at the beginning of a row or round means that the turning or starting chain contains three chain stitches which are counted as the equivalent of one treble crochet stitch. A chain may be longer than the number required for the stitch and in that case, counts as one stitch plus a number of chains. For example, *5ch (counts as 1tr, 2ch)* means that the chain is the equivalent of one treble crochet stitch plus two chain stitches.

At the end of the row or round, the final stitch is usually worked into the turning or starting chain worked on the previous row or round. The final stitch may be worked into the top chain of the turning or starting chain or into another specified stitch of the chain. For example, *1tr into 3rd of 5ch* means that the final stitch is a treble crochet stitch and is worked into the 3rd stitch of the turning or starting chain.

The box below shows the correct number of chain stitches needed to make a turn for each stitch.

DOUBLE CROCHET STITCH (dc) – 1 CHAIN TO TURN

HALF TREBLE CROCHET STITCH (htr) – 2 CHAINS TO TURN

TREBLE CROCHET STITCH (tr) – 3 CHAINS TO TURN

DOUBLE TREBLE CROCHET STITCH (dtr) – 4 CHAINS TO TURN

Stitches

Working a slip stitch (ss)

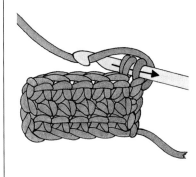

Slip stitch is the shortest of all the crochet stitches and its main uses are for joining rounds, making seams, and carrying the hook and yarn from one place to another. Insert the hook from front to back into the required stitch. Wrap the yarn over the hook (*yarn over*) and draw it through both the work and the loop on the hook. One loop remains on the hook and one slip stitch has been worked.

Working a double crochet (dc)

1 Begin with a foundation chain and insert the hook from front to back into the second chain from the hook. Wrap the yarn over the hook (*yarn over*) and draw it through the first loop, leaving two loops on the hook.

2 To complete the stitch, yarn over and draw it through both loops on the hook, leaving one loop on the hook. Continue in this way, working one double crochet into each chain.

3 At the end of the row, turn, work one chain for the turning chain (remember that this chain does not count as a stitch). Insert the hook into the first double crochet at the beginning of the row. Work a double crochet into each stitch of the previous row, being careful to work the final stitch into the last stitch of the row, but not into the turning chain.

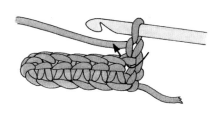

Working a half treble crochet (htr)

1 Begin with a foundation chain, wrap the yarn over the hook (*yarn over*) and insert the hook into the third chain from the hook.

2 Draw the yarn through the chain, leaving three loops on the hook. Yarn over and draw through all three loops on the hook, leaving one loop on the hook. One half treble stitch complete.

3 Continue along the row, working one half treble crochet into each chain. At the end of the row, work two chains to turn. Miss the first stitch and work a half treble crochet into each stitch made on the previous row. At the end of the row, work the last stitch into the top of the turning chain.

Working a treble crochet (tr)

1 Begin with a foundation chain, wrap the yarn over the hook and insert the hook into the fourth chain from the hook.

2 Draw the yarn through the chain, leaving three loops on the hook. Yarn over again and draw the yarn through the first two loops on the hook, leaving two loops on the hook.

3 Yarn over and draw the yarn through the two loops on the hook leaving one loop on the hook. One treble crochet complete. Continue along the row, working one treble crochet stitch into each chain. At the end of the row, work three chains to turn. Miss the first stitch and work a treble crochet into each stitch made on the previous row. At the end of the row, work the last stitch into the top of the turning chain.

Working a double treble crochet (dtr)

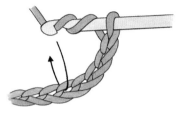

1 Begin with a foundation chain, wrap the yarn over the hook twice (*yarn over twice*) and insert the hook into the fifth chain from the hook.

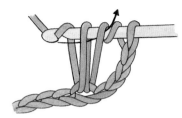

2 Draw the yarn through the chain, leaving four loops on the hook. Yarn over again and draw the yarn through the first two loops on the hook, leaving three loops on the hook.

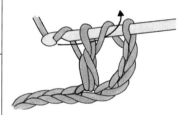

3 Yarn over again and draw through the first two loops on the hook leaving two loops on the hook.

4 Yarn over again and draw through the two remaining loops, leaving one loop on the hook. One double treble crochet complete.

5 Continue along the row, working one double treble crochet stitch into each chain. At the end of the row, work four chains to turn. Miss the first stitch and work a double treble crochet into each stitch made on the previous row. At the end of the row, work the last stitch into the top of the turning chain.

Working into the front and back of stitches

Unless pattern details instruct you otherwise, it's usual to work crochet stitches under both loops of the stitches made on the previous row.

WORKING INTO FRONT

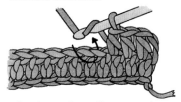

WORKING INTO BACK

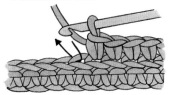

When instructions tell you to work into the front of the stitches, insert the hook only under the front loops of stitches on the previous row.

Likewise, to work into the back of the stitches, insert the hook only under the back loops of stitches on the previous row.

Tension

Each of the blocks shown in the book measures 15cm (6″) across after blocking. They were all worked using the same weight of yarn (DK) and the same hook (4mm Inox hook). No two people will crochet to exactly the same tension, even working with the identical hook and yarn. How you hold the hook and the rate at which the yarn flows through your fingers will affect the tension you produce.

To check your own tension, make a sample block using the recommended weight of yarn and the same size hook. Measure the block. It should be slightly smaller than 15cm (6″) across so that when it is blocked, it will be exactly 15cm (6″) square. As a rule, if your block is smaller than required, make another sample using a hook one size larger. Also do this when the crochet fabric feels tight and hard. If your block is larger than required, make another sample using a hook one size smaller. Also do this if the crochet fabric feels loose and floppy. Tension can also be affected by the colour and fibre composition of the yarn and the size and brand of the crochet hook, so you may need to make several blocks using different hooks until you're happy with the size and feel of your crochet fabric.

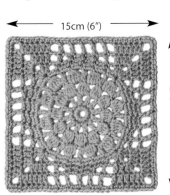

← 15cm (6″) →

15cm (6″)

Joining yarns

Some of the instructions in the book, especially for those blocks worked in rounds, will tell you exactly where to join the next yarn. For example, *Join yarn B to any tr* along one side of the block means you should join the next yarn colour to any of the treble crochet stitches along one side of the block worked on the previous row.

To do this, insert the hook in the work as instructed and draw up a loop of the new colour, leaving a tail of about 10cm (4″). Work one chain and continue with the new yarn. When instructed to *Join yarn B* without being given a specific position, you should join the new yarn where the old ends.

Changing colours

1 To make a neat join between colours, leave the last stitch of the old colour incomplete so there are two loops on the hook and wrap the new colour around the hook.

2 Draw the new colour through to complete the stitch and continue working in the new colour. The illustrations show a colour change in a row of treble crochet stitches—the method is the same for double crochet and other stitches.

Fastening off yarn

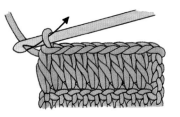

To fasten off the yarn at the end of the block, cut the yarn 15cm (6″) from the last stitch and pull the yarn end through the loop on the hook. Gently pull the yarn end to tighten the loop. To finish off yarn ends, thread the end in a large tapestry needle. Weave the end through several stitches on the wrong side of the work. Trim the remaining yarn.

Textured stitches

Working clusters (cl)

Multiples of double, half treble and treble crochet stitches can be joined into clusters by leaving the last loop of each stitch on the hook as it is made, then securing the loops together at the end. When working a beginning cluster, count the turning chain as the first stitch.

1 To work a three treble crochet cluster, yarn over hook, work the first stitch, omitting the last stage to leave two loops on the hook. Work the second stitch in the same way. You now have three loops on the hook. Work the last stitch of the cluster in the same way, resulting in four loops on the hook. Wrap the yarn over the hook.

2 Draw the yarn through the four loops on the hook to complete the cluster and secure the loops.

Working puff stitches (pf)

A puff stitch is a cluster of half treble stitches worked in the same place—the number of stitches in each puff can vary between three and five. When working a beginning puff stitch, count the turning chain as the first stitch.

1 Wrap the yarn over the hook, insert the hook into the stitch, yarn over hook again and draw a loop through (three loops on the hook). Repeat this step twice more, inserting the hook into the same stitch (seven loops on the hook).

2 Wrap the yarn over the hook and draw it through all seven loops on the hook. Work an extra chain stitch at the top of the puff to complete the stitch.

Working bobbles (b)

A bobble is a cluster of between three and five treble crochet stitches worked into the same stitch and closed at the top. Bobbles are worked on wrong side rows and they are usually surrounded by shorter stitches to throw them into high relief. When working contrasting bobbles, use a separate length of yarn to make each bobble, carrying the main yarn across the back of the bobble.

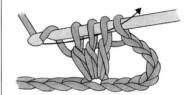

To make a three stitch bobble, wrap the yarn over the hook, work the first stitch, omitting the last stage to leave two loops on the hook. Work the second and third stitches in the same way. You now have four loops on the hook. Wrap the yarn over the hook and draw it through the four loops to secure them and complete the bobble.

Working popcorns (pc)

A popcorn stitch is a cluster of treble crochet stitches (the number may vary), which is folded and closed at the top. When working a beginning popcorn, count the turning chain as the first stitch.

1 To make a popcorn with four stitches, work a group of four treble crochet stitches into the same place.

2 Take the hook out of the working loop and insert it under both loops of the first treble crochet in the group. Pick up the working loop with the hook and draw it through to fold the group of stitches and close it at the top.

Working around the post

This technique creates raised stitches by inserting the hook around the post (stem) of the stitch below, from the front or the back.

FRONT POST TREBLE CROCHET (fptr)

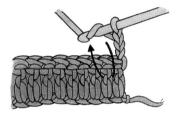

Wrap the yarn over the hook from back to front (*yo*), insert the hook from the front to the back at right of the next stitch, then bring it to the front at the left of the same stitch. Complete the stitch in the usual way.

BACK POST TREBLE CROCHET (bptr)

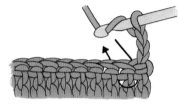

Wrap the yarn over the hook, insert the hook from the back to the front at right of the next stitch, then take it back again at the left of the same stitch. Complete the stitch in the usual way.

Working spike stitches

Spikes are made by inserting the hook one or more rows below the previous row, either directly below the next stitch or to the right or left.

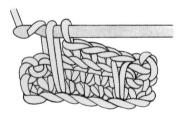

To work a double crochet spike stitch, insert the hook as directed by the pattern, wrap the yarn over the hook and draw through, lengthening the loop to the height of the working row, then complete the stitch.

Decreases

One or two stitches can be decreased by working two or three incomplete stitches together—the method is the same for double, half treble, treble, and double treble crochet stitches.

DECREASING ONE STITCH BY WORKING TWO STITCHES TOGETHER (tr2tog)

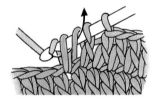
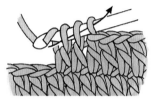

1 Leave the first stitch incomplete so there are two loops on the hook. Insert the hook into the next stitch and work another incomplete stitch so you have three loops on the hook.

2 Wrap the yarn over the hook and draw through all three loops to finish the decrease.

Two stitches can be decreased in the same way by working three stitches together. When working in treble crochet, this decrease is called *tr3tog*.

Working a diagonal decrease

This type of decrease is usually worked in the centre of the row of treble crochet to create a diagonal line of decreases. Work to the centre three stitches, miss the first stitch, work into the second stitch in the usual way, miss the third stitch, then complete the rest of the row.

Three-dimensional motifs

Initially, three-dimensional flower motifs seem a little tricky to work until you get the hang of holding the previously worked petals out of the way so you can work the foundation chains for the next layer directly behind them. This is one of those "practice makes perfect" techniques so don't give up if your first few rows of petals don't look very neat. Try using a size smaller hook to work the chains, then change back to the normal size when making the petals. This makes it easier to insert the hook between the petals when joining the chains.

Working colourwork patterns from a chart

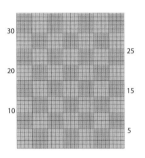

Begin by working the foundation chain in the first colour, then work the pattern starting at the bottom right-hand corner of the chart, joining in new colours as they occur on the chart. See page 117 for how to join in a new yarn. On the first row, work the first stitch into the second chain from the hook, then work the rest of the row in double crochet. Each square on the chart represents one stitch and you should always work upward from the bottom of the chart, reading odd-numbered rows (right side rows) from right to left and even-numbered rows (wrong side rows) from left to right.

When changing yarns, carry the yarn not in use loosely across the back of the work and pick it up again when it is needed. This is called stranding and it works well when the areas of colour are narrow, but when areas are wider than six stitches, use a small ball of yarn to work each colour, looping the old yarn around the new one at each changeover on the row to avoid holes.

Working in rounds

Blocks worked in rounds are worked outward from a central ring of chains called a foundation ring.

Making a foundation ring

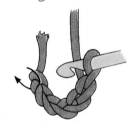

Work a short length of foundation chain (page 114) as specified in the pattern. Join the chains into a ring by working a slip stitch into the first stitch of the foundation chain.

Working into the ring

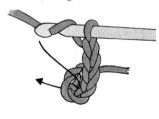

1 Work the number of turning chains specified in the pattern—three chains are shown here (counting as a treble crochet stitch). Inserting the hook into the space at the centre of the ring each time, work the number of stitches specified in the pattern into the ring. Count the stitches at the end of the round to check you have worked the correct number.

2 Join the first and last stitches of the round together by working a slip stitch into the top of the turning chain.

Finishing off the final round

To make a neat edge, finish off the final round by using this method of sewing the first and last stitches together in preference to the slip stitch joining method shown left.

1 Cut the yarn, leaving an end of about 10cm (4") and draw it through the last stitch. With right side facing, thread the end in a large tapestry needle and take it under both loops of the stitch next to the turning chain.

2 Pull the needle through and insert it into the centre of the last stitch of the round. On the wrong side, pull the needle through to complete the stitch, adjust the length of the stitch to close the round, then weave in the end on the wrong side in the usual way.

Blocking

Blocking involves pinning blocks out to the correct size, then, depending on the yarn fibre content, either steaming them with an iron or moistening with cold water. Always be guided by the information given on the ball band of your yarn and, when in doubt, choose the cold water blocking method below.

To block the pieces, make a blocking board by securing one or two layers of quilter's wadding, covered with a sheet of cotton fabric, over a 60 x 90cm (24" x 36") piece of flat board. Use a pencil to mark out a series of squares exactly 15cm (6") square on the fabric, allowing about 2.5cm (1") space between them.

the block into shape before inserting each pin.

To block woollen yarns with warm steam, hold a steam iron set at the correct temperature for the yarn about 2cm (³⁄₄") above the surface of the block and allow the steam to penetrate for several seconds. Lay the board flat and allow the block to dry completely before removing the pins.

To block acrylic and wool/acrylic blend yarns, pin out the pieces as above, then use a spray bottle to mist the crochet with cold water until it is moist, but not saturated. Gently pat the crochet to help the moisture penetrate more easily. Lay the board flat and allow the crochet to dry completely before removing the pins.

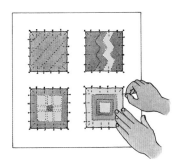

Pin out several blocks at the same time, using plenty of pins. Gently ease

Joining blocks

Blocks can be joined either by sewing or by crocheting them together with a hook. Always block the pieces before joining and use the same yarn for joining as you used for working the blocks.

Begin by laying out the blocks in the correct order with the right or wrong side of each one facing upward, depending on the joining method you have chosen. Working first in horizontal rows, join the blocks

together, beginning with the top row. Repeat until all the horizontal edges are joined. Turn the work so the remaining edges of the blocks are now horizontal and, as before, join these edges together.

Seams

Working a woven seam

Lay the blocks out with the edges touching and wrong sides facing upward. Using matching yarn threaded in a tapestry needle, weave around the centres of the stitches as shown, without pulling the stitches too tightly. Work in the same way when joining row ends.

Working a back stitch seam

Hold the blocks to be joined with right sides together, pinning if necessary. Using matching yarn threaded in a tapestry needle, work a back stitch seam along the edge.

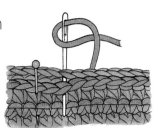

Working a slip stitch seam

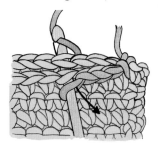

Joining blocks with wrong sides together gives a firm seam with an attractive ridge on the right side. If you prefer the ridge not to be visible, join the blocks with right sides together so the ridge is on the wrong side. Work a row of slip stitch (page 115) through both loops of each block. When working this method along side edges of blocks worked in rows, work enough evenly-spaced stitches so the seam is not too tight.

Working a double crochet seam

Work as for the slip stitch seam above, but work rows of double crochet stitches from the right or wrong side, depending on your preference.

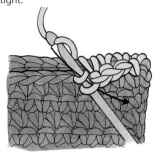

Edgings

Working directly into the afghan edge

Double crochet edging is worked directly into the crochet fabric, unlike the other edgings shown here which are worked separately and then stitched or crocheted in place. Work one or more rounds of double crochet edging right round your afghan. You can change the yarn colour at the end of every round if you want to make a striped border.

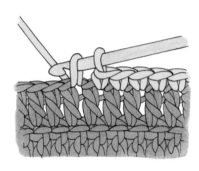

Holding the afghan with the right side facing you, make a row of ordinary double crochet stitches into the edge, spacing the stitches evenly all the way round and working three stitches into each corner stitch. When working this edging around blocks with chain spaces round the edge, work one double crochet into the chain space for every chain. Join the round with a slip stitch into the first double crochet. To work the next and subsequent rounds, work one chain, then work one double crochet into each stitch of the previous round, working three stitches into the centre stitch of each three-stitch corner group.

Working a separate decorative edging

The decorative edgings shown here are worked in rows across the width of the strip so you can make them any length by simply repeating the pattern as many times as you require. Make the strip long enough to go around your afghan, allowing extra to gather or pleat around the corners so the edging will lay flat when it is attached. Pin the edging in place, making sure that the corners are neat, choose a matching yarn colour and stitch or crochet it in place.

Shamrock edging

FOUNDATION CHAIN: Work 9ch.

FOUNDATION ROW: *(wrong side)* 1tr into 4th ch from hook, 1tr into each of next 2ch, 2ch, miss next 2ch, *(1tr into last ch, 2ch)* 3 times, 1tr into same ch, turn.

ROW 1: 1ch, [1dc, 2tr, 1dc] into first 2ch sp, [1dc, 3tr, 2ch, 3tr, 1dc] into next 2ch sp, [1dc, 2tr, 1dc] into next 2ch sp, 2ch, 1tr into each of next 3tr, 1tr into top of turning ch, turn.

ROW 2: 3ch *(counts as 1tr)*, 1tr into each of next 3tr, 2ch, [1tr, 2ch into next 2ch sp] 3 times, 1tr into same sp, turn

Rep rows 1 and 2 for desired length, ending with a second row.

Fasten off yarn.

Deep mesh edging

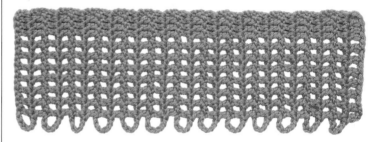

FOUNDATION CHAIN: Work 20ch.

FOUNDATION ROW: *(right side)* 1tr into 4th ch from hook, 1tr into each of next 2ch, * 1ch, miss 1ch, 1tr into next ch; rep from * to end, turn.

ROW 1: 7ch, 1tr into first tr, [1ch, 1tr into next tr] 7 times, 1tr into each of next 2tr, 1tr into top of turning ch, turn.

ROW 2: 3ch *(counts as 1tr)*, 1tr into each of next 3tr, * 1ch, 1tr into next tr; rep from * to end, turn.

Rep rows 1 and 2 for desired length, ending with a first row.

Fasten off yarn.

Scallop edging

FOUNDATION CHAIN: Work 5ch.

FOUNDATION ROW: *(wrong side)* [3tr, 3ch, 3tr] into 5th ch from hook, turn.

ROWS 1 & 2: 3ch, [3tr, 3ch, 3tr] into 3ch sp, turn.

ROW 3: 5ch, [3tr, 3ch, 3tr] into 3ch sp, turn.

ROW 4: 3ch, [3tr, 3ch, 3tr] into 3ch sp, 2ch, [1tr into 5ch sp, 2ch] 5 times, [1tr, 1dc] into next 3ch sp, turn, 3ch, 2tr into next 2ch sp, * ss into next 2ch sp, 3ch, 2tr into same sp; rep from * 3 times, 1dc into next 2ch sp, 3ch, [3tr, 3ch, 3tr] into next 3ch sp, turn.

ROW 5: 3ch, [3tr, 3ch, 3tr] into 3ch sp, turn.

ROW 6: 5ch, [3tr, 3ch, 3tr] into 3ch sp, turn.

Rep rows 4 to 6 for desired length, ending with a fourth row, omitting instructions after working 1dc into 2ch sp.

Do not break yarn.

Turn edging so RS is facing, scallops are along bottom edge and beg working across top of edging.

NEXT ROW: * 3ch, 3dc into next 3ch sp; rep from * to end, working last 3dc into top of beg 5ch, turn.

NEXT ROW: 1ch, 1dc into each dc of previous row, working 3dc into each 3ch sp, turn

NEXT ROW: 1ch, 1dc into each dc of previous row.

Fasten off yarn.

Shell & lace edging

FOUNDATION CHAIN: Work 12ch.

FOUNDATION ROW: *(right side)* 4tr into 4th ch from hook, 3ch, miss 3ch, 4tr into next ch, 3ch, miss 3ch, 1tr into last ch, turn.

ROW 1: 6ch, 4tr into first st of first 4tr group, 3ch, 4tr into first st of next group, turn.

ROW 2: 3ch, 4tr into first st of first 4tr group, 3ch, 4tr into first st of next group, 3ch, 1tr into 3rd of 6ch, turn.

Rep rows 1 and 2 for desired length, ending with a second row.

Fasten off yarn.

Making a fringe

You can make a fringe directly into the afghan edge or first work one or more rows of double crochet edging round the afghan to give a firm edge.

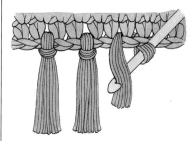

Cut the yarn twice the required length of the fringe plus about 5cm (2") extra. Take four or more lengths and fold in half. Insert a large hook through the crochet edge from back to front and draw the folded end of the yarn through to make a loop. Hook the ends through the loop and gently tighten the knot. Repeat at regular intervals along the crochet edge, then trim the ends evenly with sharp scissors.

Narrow shell edging

FOUNDATION RING: Work 4ch and join with ss to form a ring.

ROW 1: *(right side)* 3ch *(counts as 1tr)*, [3tr, 2ch, 4tr] into ring, turn.

ROW 2: 3ch, [3tr, 2ch, 3tr] into 2ch sp, 1tr into top of turning chain, turn.

Rep row 2 for desired length.

Fasten off yarn.

Abbreviations

Standard crochet abbreviations

alt	alternate
beg	beginning
ch(s)	chain(s)
cont	continue
dc	double crochet
dtr	double treble crochet
foll	following
htr	half treble crochet
lp(s)	loop(s)
patt	pattern
rem	remaining
rep	repeat
ss	slip stitch
sp(s)	space(s)
st(s)	stitch(es)
tr	treble crochet
yo	yarn over

Special abbreviations

beg cl	beginning cluster made from 3 tr sts
beg pc	beginning popcorn made from 3 ch and 4 tr sts
beg pf	beginning puff st of htr3tog
bpdc	back post double crochet
bptr	back post treble crochet
cl	cluster made from 4 tr sts
dc3tog	decrease 2 sts by working the next three dc together
dtr2tog	work 2 dtr together
fptr	front post treble crochet
MB	make bobble (work 4 open tr in same st leaving 5 loops on hook, draw yarn through all 5 loops at once)
pc	popcorn made from 5 tr sts
pf	puff st of htr4tog
sp	spike (insert hook 1 row below next st, pull up loop of yarn, insert hook into top of next st, yo, draw loop through, yo, draw through all 3 loops on hook)
tr2tog	work 2 treble crochet sts together to make cluster

Useful hook/yarn combinations

4ply (sport weight): 2.5-3.5mm (B-E)
DK (double knitting): 3.5-4.5mm (E-G)
Aran (worsted weight): 5-6mm (I-J)

Yarns

Choosing yarns

Each block in the book can be worked with your own choice of yarn. As well as using different colours (see pages 20 and 21 for more information on choosing colour combinations), fibre composition is also a choice you have to make. Pure wool yarns are considered preferable when crocheting, but there are times when synthetic yarns are better, particularly for baby items that may require frequent washing. You might also prefer the feel of an acrylic or wool/acrylic blend when you are working. The choice is up to you.

The swatches show block 173 Big Round, (page 102), worked in three different yarn weights. By using different yarns, the appearance of the block changes considerably, from light and lacy to thick and chunky. Swatch 1 is worked in Rowan 4ply Soft using a 3mm Inox hook and, after blocking, the swatch measures 11.5cm (4½") across. The next swatch is worked in Jaeger Matchmaker Double Knitting which is the same weight as the yarns used to make all the blocks in the directory. Worked with a 4mm Inox hook, the swatch measures 15cm (6") across after blocking. The last and largest swatch is worked in Jaeger Matchmaker Aran with a 5mm Inox hook and, after blocking, it measures 19.5cm (7¾") across.

Calculating yarn amounts

The most reliable way to work out how much yarn you need to buy for a specific project is to buy a ball of each yarn you are going to use for your project and make some sample swatches. The amount of yarn per ball or skein can vary considerably between colours of the same yarn because of the different dyes that have been used, so it's a good idea to make the samples using the actual colours you intend to use. Using the yarn and a suitable size of hook (see page 124 for a yarn/hook compatibility chart), work three blocks in each pattern you intend to use, making sure that you allow at least 8cm (3") of spare yarn at every colour change. This will compensate for the extra yarn you'll need when weaving in the ends.

Pull out the three blocks and carefully measure the amount of yarn used for each colour in each block. Take the average yardage and multiply it by the number of blocks you intend to make. Don't forget to add extra yarn to your calculations for joining the blocks together and for working any edgings.

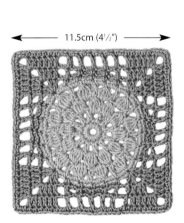

11.5cm (4½")

Worked in Rowan 4ply Soft
using a 3mm Inox hook

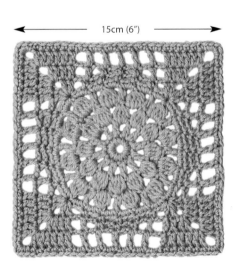

15cm (6")

Worked in Jaeger Matchmaker Double Knitting
using a 4mm Inox hook

19.5cm (7¾")

Worked in Jaeger Matchmaker Aran
using a 5mm Inox hook

Yarn colours

When creating the blocks in this book, colours were chosen from a wide palette of over seventy shades of double knitting (DK weight) yarn. Here's a list of the actual yarns used, arranged by colour. Most of the yarns are made from pure wool, but where the exact shade was unavailable in a woollen yarn, a small number of acrylics and wool/acrylic blends in the same weight were used.

white King Cole Anti-Tickle Merino DK shade "White" (blocks 25, 26, 27, 28, 65, 66, 67, 68, 169)

cream Jaeger Matchmaker DK shade 662 or King Cole Anti-Tickle Merino DK shade "Aran" (blocks 7, 9, 12, 16, 24, 38, 39, 40, 46, 47, 69, 77, 78, 91, 93, 94, 95, 103, 108, 131, 132, 135, 139, 148, 150, 154, 165, 169, 174, 178, 182, 187, 193, 196, 208, 211)

oatmeal Jaeger Matchmaker Merino DK shade 663 (blocks 48, 70, 93, 102, 106, 110, 114, 139, 141, 145, 179, 194, 200, 204, 207)

acid lemon Jaeger Matchmaker DK shade 895 (blocks 5, 30, 31, 53, 54, 61, 63, 81, 84, 85, 88, 161, 170, 194)

pale yellow Jaeger Baby Merino DK shade 205 (blocks 45, 97, 100, 136, 140, 163, 166, 170, 194, 209)

sunshine yellow King Cole Anti-Tickle Merino DK shade "Gold" (blocks 48, 49, 50, 51, 52, 76, 87, 112, 116, 133, 137, 166, 170, 183, 186, 190, 194, 200, 204, 205, 209)

amber King Cole Anti-Tickle Merino DK shade "Amber" (blocks 45, 48, 63, 64, 70, 127, 131, 151, 155, 170, 190, 200, 204)

sand Sirdar Legend DK shade 666 (blocks 102, 106, 169)

camel Debbie Bliss Merino DK shade 255103 (blocks 38, 39, 40, 69, 95, 102, 150, 154, 165, 179, 184, 193)

mustard Jaeger Matchmaker DK shade 862 (blocks 1, 2, 3, 46, 61, 62, 63, 71, 76, 94, 155)

light orange King Cole Big Value DK shade "Inca" (blocks 13, 16)

orange Jaeger Matchmaker DK shade 898 (blocks 1, 18, 20, 48, 49, 50, 61, 62, 63, 73, 74, 76, 96, 136, 140, 166, 170, 190, 200, 205, 209)

burnt orange Jaeger Extra Fine Merino DK shade 979 (blocks 3, 12, 95, 127, 131, 151, 155, 193, 209)

salmon King Cole Anti-Tickle Merino DK shade "Salmon" (blocks 9, 11, 58, 60, 91, 117, 121, 141, 145, 192, 196, 198, 202, 207, 211)

pale coral Jaeger Matchmaker DK shade 881 (blocks 12, 57, 58, 59, 92, 117, 121, 128, 132, 192, 198, 202, 211)

coral King Cole Anti-Tickle Merino DK shade "Coral" (blocks 59, 60, 89, 90, 172)

dark coral Jaeger Matchmaker DK shade 870 (blocks 9, 12, 59, 60, 91, 110, 114, 117, 120, 121, 128, 132, 192, 196, 198, 207, 211)

scarlet Jaeger Extra Fine Merino DK shade 985 or King Cole Anti-Tickle Merino DK shade "Scarlet" (blocks 13, 15, 25, 26, 27, 28, 49, 50, 75, 126, 130)

cherry King Cole Anti-Tickle Merino DK shade "Cherry" (blocks 65, 66, 67, 68, 149, 153)

raspberry Jaeger Extra Fine Merino DK shade 943 (blocks 1, 13, 15, 73, 76, 149, 153)

light raspberry King Cole Anti-Tickle Merino DK shade "Raspberry" (blocks 77, 78, 119, 120, 123, 153, 178, 208)

dark raspberry Patons Diploma DK shade 06139 (blocks 33, 36, 77, 212)

lderberry Jaeger Extra Fine Merino DK shade 944 (blocks 73, 75, 109, 113, 125, 129, 132, 140, 149, 153, 180)

pale pink Jaeger Baby Merino DK shade 221 (blocks 33, 35, 36, 77, 80, 97, 98, 103, 108, 119, 123, 125, 129, 130, 178, 212)

variegated pale pink Jaeger Baby Merino DK shade 212 (blocks 78, 164, 174, 178, 212)

dusk pink Jaeger Matchmaker DK shade 863 (block 59)

dawn pink Jaeger Matchmaker DK shade 883 (blocks 42, 44, 111, 115, 160, 171, 195)

clover pink King Cole Anti-Tickle Merino DK shade "Dusky Pink" or Patons Diploma DK shade 06158 (blocks 14, 15, 33, 36, 86)

fuchsia Jaeger Matchmaker DK shade 896 (blocks 33, 34, 83, 88, 109, 113, 125, 126, 129, 130, 140, 143, 147, 168, 172, 185, 197)

variegated fuchsia Jaeger Baby Merino DK shade 193 (blocks 35, 86, 87, 144, 148)

cyclamen pink King Cole Big Value DK shade "Fiesta" (blocks 13, 15)

magenta Jaeger Matchmaker DK shade 887 (blocks 13, 15, 33, 35, 36, 119, 124, 144, 148, 168, 172, 181, 185)

bright aubergine Jaeger Matchmaker DK shade 894 (blocks 33, 88, 110, 114, 119, 123, 181, 185)

dark aubergine Jaeger Matchmaker 4ply shade 701 used double (blocks 181, 185)

amethyst Jaeger Matchmaker DK shade 897 (blocks 15, 16, 43, 44, 107, 111, 115, 125, 129, 138, 144, 148, 160, 164, 171, 181, 191, 197, 201, 208, 212)

antique violet Jaeger Matchmaker DK shade 626 (blocks 191, 195, 197, 201)

dark violet Debbie Bliss Merino DK shade 225605 (blocks 49, 50, 126, 151, 155, 171, 180)

lavender Jaeger Matchmaker DK shade 888 (blocks 41, 42, 43, 44, 77, 79, 84, 111, 115, 118, 120, 122, 124, 143, 147, 160, 164, 167, 171, 172, 176, 180, 195)

mauve Jaeger Matchmaker DK shade 882 (blocks 44, 97, 100, 103, 108, 167, 171, 191, 197, 201)

variegated purple Jaeger Baby Merino DK shade 194 (blocks 44, 144, 148, 171, 195)

dark purple Cygnet Superwash DK shade 2999or Jaeger Matchmaker DK shade 856 (blocks 42, 44, 119, 126, 130, 167, 171)

blackberry Jaeger Extra Fine Merino DK shade 945 (blocks 21, 22, 49, 50, 81, 84, 105, 112, 118, 122, 143, 147, 159, 163, 171, 176, 180, 206, 210)

pale blue King Cole Anti-Tickle Merino DK shade "Sky Blue" (blocks 24, 53, 108, 112, 116)

variegated blue Jaeger Baby Merino DK shade 213 (blocks 21, 22, 81, 187, 206, 210)

sky blue Jaeger Matchmaker DK shade 864 (blocks 7, 8, 21, 83, 84, 97, 99, 134, 142, 146, 182, 210)

powder blue Debbie Bliss Merino DK shade 225213 (blocks 159, 163, 177)

marina blue Jaeger Extra Fine Merino DK shade 986 (blocks 18, 20, 84, 138, 162, 168, 172, 173, 177, 196, 199, 203)

mid blue Jaeger Matchmaker DK shade 889or King Cole Anti-Tickle Merino DK shade "Bluebell" (blocks 21, 22, 23, 24, 29, 32, 54, 56, 81, 82, 101, 105, 112, 116, 120, 124, 134, 138, 159, 182, 187, 198, 202, 206, 210)

cornflower blue Sirdar Wash 'N' Wear DK shade 300 (blocks 5, 6, 7, 21, 101, 105, 152, 156)

larkspur King Cole Anti-Tickle Merino DK shade "Larkspur" (blocks 83, 142, 146)

royal King Cole Anti-Tickle Merino DK shade "Royal" (blocks 21, 49, 50, 51, 65, 66, 67, 68, 152, 156, 172)

Capri blue Debbie Bliss Merino DK shade 255202 (blocks 91, 104, 177, 183, 196)

denim blue Jaeger Matchmaker DK shade 629 (blocks 21, 29, 53, 55, 182, 187)

petrol blue Patons Diploma DK shade 06212 (blocks 9, 29, 104, 107, 118, 122, 157, 161, 183, 186)

pale turquoise Jaeger Matchmaker DK shade 884 (blocks 5, 7, 9, 10, 11, 18, 20, 43, 89, 97, 100, 103, 104, 111, 117, 121, 138, 146, 158, 162, 173, 177, 183, 186, 194)

mid turquoise King Cole Anti-Tickle Merino DK shade "Turquoise" (blocks 17, 61, 63, 91, 101, 104, 107, 117, 118, 120, 124, 143, 147, 183)

variegated turquoise Jaeger Baby Merino DK shade 192 (block 186)

bright jade King Cole Anti-Tickle Merino DK shade "Green Ice" (blocks 5, 7, 53, 55, 89, 90, 156, 182)

emerald King Cole Anti-Tickle Merino DK shade "Emerald" (blocks 25, 27, 28, 49, 50, 51, 172)

grass green Cygnet Superwash DK shade 2817 (blocks 152, 156)

linden green King Cole Anti-Tickle Merino DK shade "Linden" (blocks 42, 58, 85, 87, 110, 115, 128, 129, 132, 141, 145, 181)

lime green Debbie Bliss Merino DK shade 225503 (blocks 101, 114, 142, 146, 157, 161, 172, 195)

pea green Patons Diploma DK shade 06125 (blocks 113, 170, 184, 188)

asparagus Jaeger Matchmaker DK shade 886 (blocks 18, 19, 20, 29, 31, 46, 54, 55, 61, 63, 78, 88, 105, 133, 137, 147, 158, 162, 184, 189, 199, 203)

sage green Jaeger Matchmaker DK shade 857 (blocks 4, 32, 107, 116, 128, 130, 131, 137, 157, 158, 170, 189, 193, 199, 203)

bronze green King Cole Anti-Tickle Merino DK shade "Bronze Green" (blocks 18, 189, 193, 199)

pine green Debbie Bliss Merino DK shade 225506 (blocks 31, 137)

olive green King Cole Anti-Tickle Merino DK shade "Olive" (blocks 3, 18, 20, 29, 31, 142, 146, 170, 188)

variegated green Jaeger Baby Merino DK shade 191 (block 188)

pale coffee Cygnet Superwash DK shade 4315 (block 169)

dark natural Jaeger Matchmaker DK shade 784 (blocks 20, 69, 70, 72, 93, 94, 175, 179)

mink King Cole Anti-Tickle Merino DK shade "Mink" (blocks 12, 39, 60, 69, 71, 94, 102, 127, 141, 145, 154, 165, 169, 175, 179, 184, 205)

cocoa Jaeger Extra Fine Merino DK shade 972 (blocks 12, 69, 127, 131, 145, 184, 188)

pale grey Jaeger Matchmaker DK shade 885 or King Cole Anti-Tickle Merino DK shade "Silver" (blocks 37, 39, 93, 106, 118, 122, 123, 139, 169)

steel grey Jaeger Matchmaker DK shade 892 (blocks 29, 106, 109, 169)

flannel grey Jaeger Matchmaker DK shade 782 (blocks 39, 40, 93, 135, 139, 150, 154)

clerical grey Jaeger Matchmaker DK shade 639 (blocks 37, 109, 113, 169)

Index

Stockists

Cygnet yarns are available from:
www.mcadirect.com

Debbie Bliss yarns – see list of UK stockists at:
www.debbiebliss.freeserve.co.uk

King Cole yarns are available directly from
the manufacturer:
www.stjohnswools.co.uk

Patons yarns are available from:
www.mcadirect.com

Rowan yarns – see list of UK stockists at:
www.knitrowan.com
Jaeger and Rowan yarns are available from:
www.buy-mail.co.uk
www.colourway.co.uk
www.mcadirect.com
www.upcountry.co.uk

Sirdar yarns – see list of UK stockists at:
www.sirdar.co.uk
Sirdar yarns are also available from:
www.ethknits.co.uk
www.knitwellwools.co.uk